QUANTUM LEAP YOUR LIFE

THE ULTIMATE GUIDE TO ACTING AS IF

JENNIFER BLANCHARD

CONTENTS

Author Jennifer Blanchard
P.O. Box 245
Le Roy, NY 14482
www.dreamlifeorbust.com

Disclaimer

The information in this book is meant for educational and entertainment purposes only. The author and publisher make no guarantees concerning the results or the level of success you may experience by following the advice and strategies contained in this book, and you accept the risk that results will differ for each individual. The stories and examples provided in this book show exceptional results, and are not intended to represent or guarantee that you will achieve the same or similar results, now or in the future.

The author and the publisher assume no responsibility for your actions or decisions, and hereby specifically disclaim any responsibility to any party for any liability, loss, risk, damage, or disruption of any kind caused by direct or indirect use and application of any of the contents of this book.

This book is not intended to be a substitute for legal, medical, psychological, accounting, or financial advice, or for direct expert assistance. If such level of assistance is required, the services of a competent professional should be sought.

The use of this book implies your acceptance of this disclaimer.

This book is dedicated to my soul sister, Alisa Divine — the best quantum leaping buddy I could ever ask for

INTRODUCTION

It was February 2016. I had just come off a year where I spent a good amount of time changing my mindset. I had even implemented a daily mindset practice that I was fully committed to. Every day, no matter what, I sat down for at least ten minutes and completed a specific mindset practice.

Things in my life were slowly starting to change as well. I was feeling better than I ever had, my business was growing, and I was believing more and more that my dreams were coming to fruition. But there was one specific dream that I really wanted to make happen: *I wanted to become a bestselling author on Amazon.*

I had no idea how I would do it. From where I was at that point, it seemed pretty impossible. I didn't think I had a big enough audience, a big enough online following, or the capability to sell enough books. I didn't know anyone else who had done it. I figured I would have to sell thousands upon thousands of books to achieve this dream. And I didn't believe it was possible for me.

But I still really, really wanted it.

Around that same time, I met an author online who had written and published forty-seven books (she's got even more now), *forty-six of which had hit number one in her category on Amazon.* Meeting her shifted something inside of me. I saw myself in this woman. She was much further along on her journey than I was, but we were similar enough as people and had similar enough dreams and ambitions, and energy that I could identify with her. And doing so caused me to have a thought I'd never had before: *if she can become a bestselling author that many times, I can do it at least once.*

That one simple thought changed everything for me. I decided that I, too, would become a bestselling author. I also decided it would happen that year.

Again, I had no clue how I was going to make this a reality. But I finally believed it was possible for me. And that was more than half the battle.

After making the decision, I asked myself: *if I knew and trusted this was really going to happen and I would become a bestselling author this year, what would I be doing?*

The answer was twofold: I would have a consistent habit of writing, and I would be writing and publishing more books. So that's exactly what I decided to do. I committed to building a habit of writing every day. I started with fifteen minutes a day and worked my way up from there. I also committed to writing and publishing nine new books that year–one per month for the rest of the year. (Yes, that may seem like a lot, but I tend to write short books. I like to keep each book focused on one specific topic or end result. And I had so many ideas that were ripe for the picking. For me, it just made sense to push myself in this way.)

Immediately I got to work on the first of the nine books. I had been running a free thirty-day challenge in my Facebook group called "Align Your Writing Habits to Success," and I thought: *what if I turn the content from that challenge into a book?* No sense in wasting the good content I had already written. I just had to put it into book format, weave it together so it flowed, and then edit it.

As I was putting this book together, an email landed in my inbox. The email subject line said: "Become A Bestselling Author This Year" (no joke). I opened the email and it turned out to be a promo for a software program that gave you insight into each of the Amazon book categories, and an estimate of how many books you'd have to sell in each category to hit number one.

I knew the bestselling author version of me would have this kind of information, so I subscribed to the software for six months. I started researching all of the different book categories that I thought my books fit into, and I discovered something that changed my outlook.

I discovered it didn't take quite as many book sales as I thought to hit number one in a category. There were some categories where selling five hundred books in a month could do the trick. Five hundred still seemed intimidating; at that time, I was only selling a handful of books every month. But it also didn't seem impossible. I was able to imagine many instances in which it could happen.

I continued working on *Align Your Writing Habits to Success*. As I finished up the book, an idea came to me. I wanted to start a mastermind for aspiring authors, and I wanted to show them how to become a bestselling author by allowing them to watch me do it, and explaining everything I did along the way. This would help me hold myself accountable, while also serving other writers.

The only problem was the name of the group. I had an idea for it bouncing around in my head, but I was afraid to call it that. The name was The Bestselling Author Mastermind. It felt right, but I also felt like I'd be lying if I called it that because I wasn't a bestselling author yet. I checked in with my personal accountability buddy, and she told me I had to use that name. We decided it was aspirational, and since I was going to become a bestselling author that year, it wasn't actually a lie to call it that.

While I was in publication mode for *Align Your Writing Habits to Success*, I launched The Bestselling Author Mastermind and thirty people signed up within twenty-four hours. It was the most successful launch I'd had in my business at that time. But I was also scared out of my mind. What if I *didn't* become a bestselling author? What if I told everyone in this group they could watch me make it happen, and then it didn't happen?

I decided to set those fears aside and trust. I had already decided I was becoming a bestselling author that year. And that was the decision. No deviating.

The group officially started on a Monday. My new book, *Align Your Writing Habits to Success*, debuted the following day, on Tuesday, and by Wednesday, the book was at number three in the "Authorship" category (books on how to become an author) on Amazon. I was shocked. Authorship was such a huge category with so many traditionally published books and authors in it. How was my little self-published book already at number three? I had no clue, but I did have another thought: *could get it to number one?*

I immediately jumped into action. I took to my Facebook page to tell everyone that my new book was at number three in my category. I told them I would love to get it all the way to number one. Then I asked that if they were interested in the topic to buy a copy for themselves or gift it to someone else, or to share my post so more people could know about the book. I also sent out one email to my email list, telling them the same thing.

The following day, my book was at number one in the "Authorship" category, and I became a bestselling author on Amazon.

My mind was blown. I had only decided four months prior that I was going to be a bestselling author, and here it was happening before my very eyes.

Not only that, but my next book, *The 15-Minute Writer*, also hit number one in the "Authorship" category, as well as in two other categories, and then it stayed at number one for an entire month! I also suddenly began selling hundreds of books every month without even trying very hard. I was making the most book sales and the most money I'd ever made from my books.

I had officially become the author I always dreamed I would be. And I've been on that same path ever since. I even had another one of my books, *The Writer's Confidence Boost*, hit number one.

I totally quantum leaped my writing career that year. Most importantly, I knew if I could do it with one thing, I could do it with everything! And I've been quantum leaping in different areas of my life ever since.

This book, *Quantum Leap Your Life*, is your go-to resource for making massive changes in your life, and at a much faster pace than is typical or logical. I'm breaking down every single piece of the quantum leaping process to show you what it is, how it works, and how to make it work for you.

So, if you're ready, turn the page, and let's do this thing!

Dream life or bust,
   jennifer

P.S. I use the phrase "the Universe" to describe the all-knowing, all-loving energy others call God or Source. Also, keep in mind that I've deliberately tried to separate each part of the quantum leaping process into chapters of this book, but all of the parts work together, so you will see some cross-referencing.

ONE

QUANTUM LEAPING

L et's start with the obvious: *what is a quantum leap?* The Merriam-Webster dictionary defines it as: "an abrupt change, sudden increase, or dramatic advance." This can be applied to anything. In manifestation, it means you make a huge jump from where you are in your life right now—or a specific area of your life—to where you desire to be. A quantum leap feels like magic, a miracle, overnight success, or instant results.

Sounds pretty good, right? Who wouldn't want to make a huge change in their life in a short period of time? Especially when there's something you're deeply desiring.

Making a quantum leap is pretty simple. It's implementing it in your own life where the challenge typically arises. And that's because we've been taught that change is hard, it takes a lot of time, and sacrifice is required. None of which is actually true, but it's what most people believe about change. Sometimes it seems easier to just stay where you are in life. You may be having a mediocre experience, but at least you're comfortable. Your life feels predictable, and that is less intimidating than surrendering to the unknown, even if the unknown means getting to have what you want.

My goal is to show you how simple, easy and even fun it can

be to make a massive and immediate up-level in your life. A quantum leap only requires three things:

- A shift in your mindset
- A shift in your energy—aka emotional state
- A shift in your actions

When you look at it in this way, it doesn't seem as scary. In fact, it makes it seem a lot more doable.

The biggest question most people have is: *how do I do it?* And while I'm not big on asking how (after all, I am the author of a book called *F*ck the How*), there are definitely specific steps you can take.

I'm going to show you from my own personal journey, learnings, and experiences how to make a quantum leap in your life. I'm going to give you as many examples as I can to illustrate all of the steps, and I'm going to answer many of the questions I think you'll have along the way.

I highly recommend you get yourself a notebook or journal (or you can use your computer). It will be super helpful to have one for completing the exercises I give you throughout the book. It's all well and good to think about the things you want or the changes you desire to make, but it's a whole other thing to start writing that stuff down. Writing it down makes it feel more real. And that's what we're going for.

The Buffet of Realities

In quantum physics, every reality and outcome, and possibility exist all at the same time. Think of it like a buffet at a restaurant, where every food option is available at once. You just choose what you want. Same with choosing your reality. This means two things:

1. **The reality you desire for yourself—in whatever area(s) you desire it in—is available to you.**
2. **Multiple realities can and will be true simultaneously.**

Your experience of reality will be different than someone else's, and both realities are real and true. If you want to quantum leap, you must accept that many realities will exist, and still continue to choose, believe in, have faith in, and take a stand for the one you want. Doing so is what makes it eventually become true.

Here's the best example I can come up with from my life to illustrate this for you: I've been divorced for almost four years (as of the writing of this book), but I've still been financially tied to my ex-husband because of some old tax debt from my business. At the time of filing those taxes, back when we were still married, we had a tax accountant who wasn't very good at his job. He didn't tell us that if you're married but one spouse owns a business, you should file your taxes "married, but separate," so the business taxes stay with the business-owning spouse and do not also become the responsibility of the non-business-owning spouse.

So, my old business taxes were tied to my ex as well, making him financially liable for them, even though the actual tax debt didn't belong to him. Worst of all, the IRS had been taking his tax refund from him every year for the past four years, to pay for my business tax debt. I'm sure you can imagine the kind of animosity that created between us.

Since all realities and outcomes and possibilities exist at the same time, I knew there could be a reality where he was relieved from my tax debt, and all of his refunds would be returned to him. It just wasn't the reality I was living yet. I continued to believe and trust in this reality.

But all of the lawyers and tax accountants I had spoken to didn't agree with my belief. Every single one of them told me I was dreaming and there was no way the IRS would ever release him from owing the tax debt, especially since we filed as "married," instead of "married filing separate" (and the IRS doesn't let you change your filing status after your taxes have been filed). The reality for those people was that there was nothing we could do about it, we just had to deal with being legally and financially stuck together until the debt was fully paid off.

But that wasn't the reality I chose for us. I chose the reality that my ex would be relieved from the tax debt and would get his refunds returned back to him. This is the reality I chose to believe in, have faith in, and take a stand for, regardless of what other people were saying. I surrendered it and held faith in this reality for over a year and a half after we filed the "Innocent Spouse" paperwork with the IRS.

And that reality became true for me. I recently received a letter from the IRS that said they made the decision to grant my now-ex-husband full relief from my old tax debt, and all of the money he paid toward the debt would be refunded to him.

This happened in spite of what's typical, and in spite of everything the experts and legal minds had to say about it, because that is the reality I continued to choose. I didn't let what they had to say taint my belief. I didn't let the reality they presented me with affect me. I just continued to choose and know and believe in the reality I wanted. Because, in the quantum, that reality existed, along with all of the other possible realities.

Choose Your Reality

"Reality" is deeply personal, and something you create for yourself with your beliefs, thoughts, feelings, and actions. And while, yes, there are some realities that exist for all, the main reason they do is because those realities have been accepted by the majority of society–and the world–as true. But if the collective decided to believe in something else, a different reality would then become possible for everyone.

So, if all realities and possibilities exist all at the same time in the quantum, what reality are you going to choose for yourself? What reality do you want to choose for the area(s) you desire a quantum leap in?

Choose it, believe in it, have faith in it, and take a stand for it, regardless of what's going on around you, what your physical reality currently says, or what other people have told you.

This is the tricky part because we've been so conditioned to think our current physical reality is the only truth that exists, and so often we're swayed off of our path by society and the people around us. In the upcoming chapters, we'll talk more about how to choose and then stick with the reality you want until you see it through to fruition.

Become A Vibrational Match

It has been proven by science that everything is made of energy —including you, your thoughts, beliefs, emotions, and actions. It may seem like you have a physical body or physical items surrounding you. It may seem like the things you see in your world are solid matter. But at a molecular level, everything that looks solid is still made of energy.

And because it's made of energy, that means it's also vibrating (this is known as the Law of Vibration). Everything made of energy vibrates, which means everything—including you—has a vibrational frequency. That frequency either attracts or repels things, based on like vibration (this is known as the Law of Attraction).

So, when two things are vibrating at the same frequency, they are attracted to each other or pulled together. And when two things are vibrating on different frequencies, they repel each other.

Think of it like a phone call. If you dial the correct number—

the phone frequency of the person you want to talk to—you reach the correct person. But if you dial a different number or mess up any of the digits in the number, you'll reach an entirely different person. And that's because a phone number is a specific frequency. It requires you to be an exact match to that frequency in order to reach the person you desire to.

Same goes for your quantum leap. You must match the vibration of the reality you desire to have in order for it to become true for you.

The reality you want already exists as a specific frequency. There's at least one person in the world who has and is living that reality. And that means it's available to you too.

So, if you want to make a quantum leap in your life, you must first know what you want, and then you must find a way to match the frequency of it. When you do, you're being a vibrational match and the thing you want can make its way into your physical reality.

Clarity Comes First

Making a decision is the starting point for the entire quantum leaping process. You can't manifest, hit your goal, create the reality, get the outcome, or make a quantum leap of any kind if you're not clear on what you want. So, we start here.

Your first step is to get clear on what you want. What reality do you want to create for yourself? What do you want your life to be like? What do you want for the various area(s) you're desiring a change in?

This is what you need to be clear on.

My recommendation is to get out that journal or notebook we talked about and do some freestyle writing around those questions. You can also make a list of every area you'd like to quantum leap in, and then journal about the reality you want to create in each of those areas.

Here are some suggested areas to consider:

- Self
- Body
- Health
- Love life
- Family
- Friends
- Lifestyle
- Money
- Business and/or career
- Giving back
- Spirituality
- Purpose and legacy

While it's totally possible to quantum leap in all of these areas at the same time, it could get overwhelming. So, it's better to choose one or two areas to start with. And sometimes, just by quantum leaping in one area, you automatically make a leap in the other areas too. This is because many areas overlap. For example, by making a quantum leap in your business or career, you're also likely to make one in your money, your purpose, and your lifestyle.

What's most important to you right now? Give yourself some time with this, so you can really feel into what matters most and what you can put on hold for a little while.

At the time of writing this book, I'm working on making a quantum leap in four areas: my writing career, my money, my lifestyle, and my ideal physical body (and also health, which goes hand-in-hand with body). A few years ago, I was working on—and then made—a quantum leap in my love life (which I talked all about in my book, F*ck the How).

So, it's really about what matters to you right now. Where would you love to see yourself at this time next year—or six months from now—if you could have anything you wanted? It's all up to you. And you always get to have what you want or something even better.

To help you get clear, here's a simple quantum leap formula you can use: *From X to Y*. For example, from having no money to five figures in the bank. From being single to having the relationship of your dreams. From being overweight to having the body you desire. From having a day job to working for yourself. You can be as specific or general as you want, whatever feels best to you.

Now Decide

You may not realize this, but there is so much power in your decision. Your decision to have something, to change your life, to choose a new reality, to make a quantum leap can and will move mountains. The problem comes in when you've got split energy.

If you're not familiar with the phrase, "split energy" is when you're constantly going back and forth on something. One minute it's this, the next minute it's that. Back and forth you go. Over and over again.

That's split energy. And split energy comes from one thing and one thing only: you haven't made a decision yet (even if you think you have).

When you make a decision, you fully back it and there's no wavering. There's no questioning. There's no contemplating other realities.

There's simply the decision you've made and you stand behind it in all ways and allow for nothing less. The way to heal split energy is to finally and fully make a decision. This is the part that's most challenging.

A question I get asked a lot by my clients is: *how do I know when I've made a decision?* There are six specific factors involved in making a decision. Those factors are:

- Desire—knowing what you want
- Belief—choosing what you believe about what you want

- Thoughts—how you're choosing to think about what you want
- Feelings—how you're choosing to feel about what you want
- Intentions—what you're intending about what you want
- Actions—how you're acting in alignment with what you want

I created a Decision Chart to show you what it looks like to make a decision, and exactly what's involved in that process. Below you'll see three pics of the Decision Chart I made. One is a blank chart, for reference. The other two show you what it looks like when you have split energy, and when you've actually made a decision.

When all six of these areas are at one hundred percent on the Decision Chart, you've made a decision. You are fully backing yourself on that decision in all ways, and you're being a vibrational match. When you haven't fully made a decision, you have split energy.

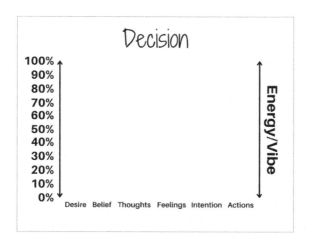

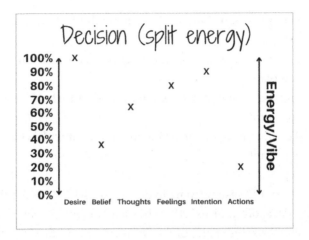

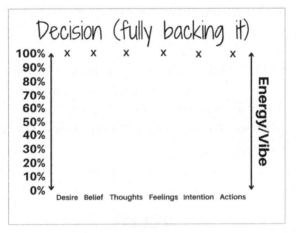

IF YOU DO CATCH yourself wavering, ask yourself: *why am I still going back and forth?* Is it because of fear? Are you doubting something? Are you "shoulding" yourself into wanting something that you don't actually want? Are you not allowing yourself or giving yourself permission to want what you truly want?

And if you're unclear on what you deeply desire at this time, I highly recommend downloading my free audio training + worksheet:

Desires vs Shoulds: www.jenniferblanchard.net/desires.

This will help you get crystal clear on what you want.

"Be" Is the Key

Now you're going to create what you want by starting from who and where you want to be, not from who and where you are right now. We're taught by other people and society that if we want something, we have to work really hard, do a lot of things, pay our dues, put in the time, sacrifice and hustle. But that is the complete opposite of how a quantum leap works. In the quantum leaping process, the paradigm is *be, do, have*. And that starts with *being* someone who has what you want, not doing things in order to earn something or make something happen.

When you know what you want, you can quantum leap your way to it by stepping into the identity of the version of you who already has it, who is already "there." Everything you want is available to you right now. But you have to first become the version of yourself who has those things in order to bring them into your life.

Being is another way of saying *identity*. When you identify as someone who has the things you want—when you are being that person in thought, feeling, belief, and action—you will get to have them.

An identity is simply how you see yourself. It's the way you think about yourself and your life. It's the beliefs you hold. It's the actions you take or don't take. It's your energy. It's your standards and boundaries. It's your personality and way of carrying yourself. It's your attitude. It's your worldview.

For most of us, our identities were created over the course of our childhoods, based on the things we experienced and what we were taught. This is why a lot of adults will say things like, "I'm exactly like my mother," or "I'm becoming my father." It's because their identity has been crafted through external circumstances and people.

But that's just one option. You can also decide to let go of the identity you were given, and create the identity you actually desire to have. You can be the version of yourself who has everything you want, in every area of your life.

If you read the Introduction to this book (and I really hope you did), I gave you an example of how I became a bestselling author on Amazon. It wasn't about the actions that I took. I didn't really take very many actions at all. It wasn't about how much time and effort I put in. From the day I decided it was going to happen to the day it actually happened was about four months. It wasn't about how much hustle I had. For my book to become a bestseller, I only put up one Facebook post and sent out one email.

But it was about who I was being. Over the course of those four months, I stepped into the identity of being a bestselling author. I had a daily habit of writing. I wrote a new book. I changed my mindset and my beliefs about myself and what was possible for me as a self-published author. I took the actions I felt inspired to and that aligned with me being a bestselling author. I took on the identity of a bestselling author. I saw myself as one. I felt like one. I believed and thought like one. So, of course, that is the reality I created.

Before I became a bestselling author, that version of me existed in the quantum. It was always a possibility that was available and there for me to choose. I just hadn't actually chosen it yet. Once I did, that's when I was ready to be that version of me, and do the things that version of me would do. And that's also when I got to have the things that version of me would have, including seeing my book at number one in my category on Amazon.

Are You Willing to Have It All?

Having it all is a topic that gets thrown around a lot in the personal development and spirituality worlds. Most of these authors and gurus are referring to the idea of getting to have everything you want. And while that's part of it, there's also another part that few people ever talk about. Because having it all means having all of it—the thing you want *and* everything else that comes with it. The good and the potential downsides.

For example, your dream lake house, and the possibility that it could get flooded. The money you want, and all of the taxes you'll have to pay. Becoming famous on Instagram, and having people make fake accounts and pretend to be you. Tens of thousands of followers on TikTok, and getting hate comments. The love of your life, and all of his really annoying habits. The baby you've always dreamed of, and all of the sleepless nights.

Having it all means being willing and able to take the good with the not-so-good. It means accepting that the thing you want may come with a potential downside and being okay with that. Pastor Michael Todd, the author of *Crazy Faith*, calls this the "backside of the blessing."

A lot of people aren't willing to have it all in this way, and that's why they energetically block the things they want from coming to them. They're actually getting something out of not receiving what they want.

So, they don't get the money they desire, but they also don't have to worry about paying the taxes on it or having people come out of the woodwork asking for a loan. They don't get the online fame that would allow them to make a living doing what they love, but they also don't have to deal with putting themselves out there, or people impersonating them or leaving rude, mean comments on their posts.

Sometimes not getting what you want is actually protecting you from the downsides.

And this is why it's so important to not only know what the potential downsides of what you want are but to also find a way to be accepting of them. If you can do that, then you'll be able to handle having it all. You have to find a way to make the good parts, the upside of the thing you want, outweigh the potential negatives.

So, what are the possible downsides that could come along with you getting to have the things that you want? Sit down, write them out in your journal and look at them. Doing this is so freeing and it will help you to make peace with it. The reason the downsides seem scary is because they're unknown. But as soon as you make them known, by looking them in the eye, it removes the emotional charge.

You have to be able to handle having what you want and everything that comes with it. Until you can do that, you will subconsciously and/or energetically block yourself from receiving it.

Overriding What Used to Be

You've likely had your current identity for a long time. Maybe months. Maybe years. Maybe your entire life. And that comes with pre-programmed thoughts, beliefs, emotions, and ways of being that may not align with who you now desire to be and what you now desire to have.

The good news is, you can override your previous identity by choosing to think, feel, believe and act like the version of yourself who has the things you want right now. And you do that by asking yourself one very important question: **if I was already that person—the one who has the things that I want— what would I be thinking, believing, feeling, and doing?**

The coming chapters will show you how to answer that question for yourself.

Killing Your Quantum Leap

There's one thing that will kill a quantum leap. And that's the phrase, "it's not working." Since you get to decide your reality and what's true for you, if you decide to tell yourself "it's not working," then it can't work. Nothing you do can make it work because that statement will energetically block it from working.

Don't do that to yourself. You deserve to make a quantum leap. You're worthy of it. It's available and yours for the taking.

When you find yourself feeling like "it's not working," you can lean on my *Four Truths of Surrender*. And those truths are:

1. **The Universe is on it the moment you decide it's yours** (or the moment you ask for it or offer gratitude in advance for it).
2. **It's working even if you can't see it with your physical senses** (especially when you can't).
3. **It's working better than you can even imagine**.
4. **For every one step you take, the Universe takes more.**

These are the truths that I live by in my own life. Whenever something happens that makes me start doubting or worrying or being in fear of not getting to have what I want, I take a deep breath and then return to these four truths.

Quantum Leap Your Life: Chapter One Recap

• **What do you want?** Take some time to journal this out and get clear on it. Here are some areas to consider:

> Self
> Body
> Health
> Love life
> Family
> Friends
> Lifestyle
> Money
> Business and career
> Giving back

> Spirituality
> Purpose and legacy

• **Are you at one hundred percent in all areas on the Decision Chart?** (Refer to the section above for more on this.) And if not, what can you do to get to one hundred percent? Remember— you must make a decision on what you want before you can make a quantum leap.

• **What reality are you going to choose for yourself?** What reality do you want to choose for the area(s) you desire a quantum leap in? You will get whatever reality you choose, put your belief and faith behind, and take a stand for.

• **Who is the version of you that already has the things you want, who has already made a quantum leap from where you are right now to where you want to be?** Freestyle journal on this.

• **What are the potential downsides of the things you currently desire to have? Write it all out and take a good look at it. Then, make a game plan.** If those things were to happen, how would you handle it? Really think about this and write out what you would do, what you could put in place, what boundaries you could set, etc. This will help you feel more confident that you can handle whatever comes your way, and will energetically open you up to receiving what you want.

Quantum Leap Your Life: Chapter One Journal Prompts

For each of these prompts, do some freestyle journaling, or answer in bullet points, whichever works best for you.

- Who do I want to be in my life?
- What would it look like for me if I felt really proud of myself?
- What does making a quantum leap mean to me?

- What reality would I choose for myself if I could have anything and there were no limits?

TWO
BELIEVING

Once you're clear on what you want and you've made a decision, next up is looking at your beliefs. A belief is just a thought or statement that you agree is true. But *how* does a belief become true?

Simple: you've thought about or experienced that thing enough times that you now accept it as truth. You have beliefs about everything–yourself, your life, your family, your friends, society, life in general, the place you grew up, your job, your mode of transportation, your clothes, your home, etc. All of these beliefs contribute to your worldview, or how you see the world and yourself in it.

Most of the beliefs you currently hold were given to you during your childhood. You've experienced many things that helped create your beliefs. And most of what you learned growing up were very limited ways of looking at yourself and the world.

The beliefs you currently hold have created your identity up to this point. And if you continue to choose to hold onto those beliefs, you will continue to uphold and maintain the identity that you're used to having.

But you're reading this book right now because you want to

make a quantum leap in your life. A lot of those old beliefs are not going to serve you going forward. If you want to become a different version of yourself, you must start by changing the beliefs you currently hold.

How Beliefs Work

A belief is only true if you decide that it is. Beliefs are fluid. And what you believe only affects what's possible for *you*. It has no bearing on anyone else. This means you can choose to believe something and someone else can choose not to believe it. In your reality, you will experience that belief, and in their reality, they will not (aside from Universal Laws, like gravity or the Law of Attraction, that apply to everyone).

So, you could choose to believe that you have to work hard for money, and that will be your experience–you will only receive money when you work really hard for it. But someone else could decide to believe money is easy, and that will be their experience–they will receive money in ways that feel easy to them. It's all about what you decide to believe in and put your faith behind.

For example, growing up, I had a belief that guys only liked blondes. I took on this belief from the movies I watched, and from being in school and seeing the guys I liked not liking me back but instead liking the girls with blonde hair. I accepted that belief as truth for myself. Now, did that actually mean it was true? Of course not. Guys like girls with all different colors of hair. But my younger self didn't experience it that way because of this belief.

After years of trying to convince my mother to let me dye my hair blonde, she finally gave in and let me get blonde highlights (I then proceeded to keep getting my hair re-highlighted until my entire head was blonde). Suddenly, my reality shifted. I had blonde hair, and because I also had a belief that guys were only attracted to girls with blonde hair, I started to get all kinds of attention from guys. I started to hear guys say things to me that they'd never said before, like "you're hot," and "you're beautiful." No one had ever said that stuff to me when I was a brunette. Not only that, I also dated a couple of the guys I really wanted to date.

But there was a huge problem with this belief that I ran into once I graduated from high school and went to college. Having blonde hair when you're naturally a brunette requires a lot of upkeep. In high school, my mom paid for me to get my hair done, but when I got to college, I was on my own. And continuing to dye my hair blonde all the time was too expensive for a broke college student. So, one day, I took my roommates to Walmart to buy blonde hair dye. I thought it might be less expensive if I did it myself. But while I was there, I found this really amazing shade of eggplant that was calling to me. I had never had red hair before (or purple, in this case). I thought it might be fun to pull a changeup and try something different.

But since I still had a belief that guys only liked blondes, I knew if I was going to dye my hair a darker color, I would also have to let go of that belief. I finally felt confident in how I looked and I constantly had guys at college telling me how hot I was. I didn't want to lose that because I changed my hair color.

So I decided to believe I was hot no matter what color my hair was, and I continued to work on believing that. It eventually stuck, and I continued to feel attractive and date the guys I wanted, even as I got into my early twenties and eventually went back to being a brunette.

This works with literally every single thing that you believe. You're only experiencing something in your reality because you're believing it—consciously or subconsciously. The belief is creating that experience and that reality for you. But you can choose at any time to believe something else. As soon as your subconscious gets the message, you will have a different experience and a reality that's more aligned with what you want.

Changing A Belief

Something to know about beliefs is they live in your subconscious mind, the part of your mind that controls your identity. It's also the part that's responsible for maintaining your bodily functions, like breathing and keeping your heart beating. This part of your mind is programmed very early on in your life, typically between birth and age seven.

Your subconscious mind is meant to be a servant to your conscious mind, doing whatever it tells it to do. Unfortunately, what happens for most people is they allow their subconscious mind to take over, and their conscious mind becomes the servant instead. Your subconscious then begins to control your life, identity, and reality by creating more of what has already been programmed in. Think of it like a MacBook–your quantum leap requires the most up-to-date version of the Apple Operating System (OS), but your subconscious mind is still running the OS from Apple-1 (the original Apple computer).

For this reason, it can be challenging to change that programming. Challenging, but not impossible. Changing a belief really only requires two things: a decision, and repetition over a period of time.

First, you have to decide that you're going to change whatever belief you have that is not serving you, and you also have to decide what the new belief you want to program in is going to be. Secondly, you must find a way to get that new belief into your subconscious mind through repetition.

There are several specific times when this reprogramming should be done for optimum results:

- First thing upon waking
- Right before you fall asleep
- After meditation
- During mindless activities that don't require you to think, like washing dishes, cleaning the house, waiting

in line at the grocery store, etc.
- While you're asleep

There are many ways to create the repetition required to reprogram your beliefs. You can write out all of the new beliefs that would allow you to create a quantum leap in your life, and then you can recite them during the optimum reprogramming times every day. You could also record yourself saying these new beliefs into an MP3 app on your phone and then listen to this audio on repeat at the optimum times, as well as all throughout the day, including when you're asleep. There's this great iPhone app called *ThinkUp* that allows you to record each belief statement separately, and then play them all together in a loop. I love this because it makes it much easier to change the belief statements whenever you want to without having to re-record the whole audio.

My favorite way to reprogram beliefs is to make a list of everything you would believe if you already had the things that you want, keep the list by your bed, and then immediately upon waking, grab it and go through each statement. Here's what I do: I read the first statement on the list out loud with my eyes open, really taking in the words on the paper. And then I close my eyes and repeat the belief statement one to three times in my head. While I'm doing this, I also try to visualize what it would look like if that statement were true, and I feel the emotion of it being true. I do this when I first wake up and again right before I go to sleep.

I also like to piggyback doing belief work with my workouts. I'll exercise for thirty to forty-five minutes, and then as a cooldown, I will sit with my eyes closed and breathe in and out slowly, while meditating on one or more of my belief statements. Over and over again, as I'm breathing in and out, I will say the words in my head, and I will feel the emotions of the words being true.

The good news is, your subconscious can't tell whether

QUANTUM LEAP YOUR LIFE   23

something is true or not. It just accepts everything as truth, so why not choose to program in beliefs that will support you in having what you want and being who you want to be?

What Would Your Beliefs Be?

Before you can reprogram any beliefs, you have to be clear on which beliefs the quantum-leaped version of you would be believing. You don't have to get this perfect, you just have to be willing to do the work and be open to shifting to beliefs that are more supportive.

So, what *would* you be believing if you already had the thing you want, or if you were already that person? The answer will depend on what you want, of course, but here are some examples to get your creative juices flowing.

Let's say you want to quantum leap and make more money in your business, or get a raise at your job. Some of the new beliefs you might decide to take on for yourself could be:

- Money comes easily to me
- Money is easy to make and receive
- Money is my friend
- Money loves me
- Customers love to pay me
- I am a money magnet
- I make thousands of dollars every month through my business
- New clients come to me with total ease every day
- My work is valuable and of high service to my company
- My boss sees my value and honors it with extra money

Or, if you want to quantum leap into the version of yourself who has the love life you desire, some new beliefs could be:

- I am loved and in love
- I am in the best relationship I've ever had
- I have the best boyfriend/girlfriend in the world
- I love myself and allow myself to be loved by another
- Love is who I am
- I am now receiving the love and relationship I desire

Or, if you want to quantum leap into the physical body you dream of, some new beliefs could be:

- I have the body of my dreams
- I love my body
- I am strong, lean, fit, toned, and healthy
- I have a hot body
- I am getting stronger, leaner, fitter, healthier, and more toned every day
- I am sexy as fuck
- I love how I feel in my body

Your New Beliefs

Now it's your turn to come up with the beliefs that the quantum-leaped version of you would have. My recommendation is to start each belief with one of the following:

- I am...
- I have...
- I love...
- I am so happy and grateful that...

These phrases are a powerful starting point for any new belief you want to create. And if you're having a hard time coming up with a set of new beliefs for yourself and/or the thing that you want, you can always ask yourself what someone else who already has this thing would be believing. This one helped me a ton when I was ready to create new beliefs around having the home I desire.

I've been dreaming of owning a lake house since I was a kid, and I finally got the internal message that it was time to manifest one (I'm working on this now). But I was feeling blocked around what beliefs I would hold, so I asked myself what someone who already owned a lake house would be believing. And the first thing that popped in my head was: *I live on the lake*. So simple, yet that was a belief I hadn't even thought of. But, of course, someone who owns a lake house would believe that they live on the lake–because they do! They might also believe things, like:

- I can afford to live on the lake
- I love living in my lake house
- I have the lake house of my dreams
- I love my vacation lifestyle
- I love living on the water
- I am so happy and grateful that I get to wake up looking at the water every day

Sometimes it can be challenging to come up with beliefs for yourself, but if you look at someone else who has what you want, it can be easier to deduce what they might be believing. And that's a good starting point for creating new beliefs for yourself.

Your Limiting Beliefs

Creating new beliefs is great, and is an important part of quantum leaping your life, but there's more to it than that. Because you can create all the new beliefs you'd like, but if you're still holding onto the old limiting beliefs, you won't get very far. Those old beliefs will constantly pull you back into your comfort zone and keep you from doing the things that will allow you to make a quantum leap. A limiting belief is a belief that limits what's possible for you.

You don't need to know every single limiting belief you have going on, just the main ones that tend to come up for you all of the time. Sometimes we think things so often we don't even realize it's a limiting belief that we're dealing with.

For example, a woman commented on one of my TikTok videos the other day, saying she wants to get married but she's forty-five and still single. Immediately I picked up on a limiting belief that she likely didn't even realize was limiting her–she believes you can't get married or find love if you're forty-five; that it's too old, or too late. Once I pointed it out to her, she was mind-blown and right away knew she had been holding herself back with that belief. Now she knows what to work on–both releasing that limiting belief, and creating a new one that's more supportive of her getting married and having the love she desires.

We all have limiting beliefs going on that are getting in the way of us having what we want, that are keeping us stuck, and making the things we desire feel impossible or unlikely. But all of that is total bullshit. You always get to have what you want, you always get to decide what you're going to believe, and only you can do that for yourself.

This is why it's just as important to look at and release any limiting beliefs you have as it is to create new ones that will help you to quantum leap your life.

How do you find some of those limiting beliefs? By answering the following two questions:

1. What do I want?
2. Why don't I have it yet?

The first question gets you clear on what you desire, and the second one shows you where all of the limiting beliefs are hanging out. Sure, you might call those things reasons or roadblocks, and they might be totally legit. But they're also stopping you from having what you want. So, you have to decide for yourself what's more important, holding onto those comfy old beliefs and stories about yourself and your life, or having what you want. You always get to choose.

When I was looking at the limiting beliefs surrounding me owning a lake house, here's what came up for me as to why I don't have it yet:

- My credit isn't good enough
- I don't have enough money for a down payment yet
- I can't afford one
- There are no good lake houses for sale where I live
- No bank will give me a loan

The crazy thing is, I had no actual idea if my credit was that bad or if a bank wouldn't give me a loan. I hadn't even tried! I just decided that was probably what would happen, and turned it into a limiting belief that stopped me from having my lake house. Most of the limiting beliefs and stories we have about ourselves, our lives, and even the world, aren't actually true. You can always look at the world at large and find someone who was an exception to every single thing you think is holding you back.

For example, there are plenty of people who have bought a house with no down payment. There are plenty of people with mediocre credit who own a lake house right now. There are many other options for having a lake house other than buying one of the ones currently for sale–like buying a plot of land on the lake and building a house or putting a modular home on it, or even renting a lake house to start with.

But when we've got limiting beliefs and stories going on, we tend not to see the other options and possibilities that are available. Or if we do see them, we come up with some lame story or limiting belief to push them away and make them not for us.

If you want to quantum leap your life, you have to be willing to look at the limiting beliefs and stories that are holding you back, and you also have to be willing to let them go. Yes, it's a process and it will take some time, but if you keep at it, eventually those old beliefs will fade and the new ones will replace them.

What Stories Have You Been Telling?

Another way to look for limiting beliefs is to look at the stories you tell. And I don't mean stories recounting specific things that actually happened in your physical reality. I'm talking about the inner stories you tell yourself or tell others about yourself. Whatever you believe is simply a story you've been telling yourself or repeating enough times that you now believe it.

For example, a very popular inner story for a lot of people is a victim story. Somewhere along your life journey, something happened to you that felt out of your control. Sometimes it's an isolated incident that you managed to let go of. Other times, you've taken it on and made it your story in life. Such as, "I'm no good at this," or "the guy I want never wants me," (this was my story around love for a long time), or "life is working against me."

Playing the victim card is really easy because it removes any responsibility from you and puts it onto someone else or life in general. But telling a victim story has no power in it. And it's a very limiting way of seeing yourself and your life.

Yes, maybe something bad did happen to you at one point, but it's your choice to continue telling that story. You could also choose to tell the story of how you now want your life to be. What happened to you is far less interesting than what you chose to do with it.

Here's a more specific example: I know a guy whose birth

parents gave him up for adoption. And he continues to live from that story to this day. His whole life is a story of him never being good enough, and it all starts with his birth parents giving him up. Rather than looking for the triumph in his story–that he was adopted by loving parents who raised him and took care of him and who have been there for him and supported him whenever he needed it–he talks about all the bad things that happened to him because his birth parents gave him up.

But what you have to see in all of this is that these are just stories. Just judgments, just perceptions, just ways of seeing yourself and your life that either serve you or don't serve you. These stories are just limiting beliefs that keep you stuck right where you are.

Whatever meaning you've given to the inner stories or limiting beliefs you have right now, you can decide to change it. You no longer have to see yourself as a victim (or whatever your story is). You can choose to see yourself in a totally different way. You can make the things that happened in your past mean something totally different.

For example, rather than making something bad that happened to you mean you're a victim, you can choose to make it mean you're a survivor, that you're brave, that you kept going and nothing could keep you down in life. That story has a much different energy and it better represents who you want to be, not who you were. Quantum leaping requires you to tell the story how you want it to be, not how it currently is or how it has been.

Before we dive into how to release your limiting beliefs, I want to add that there's no judgment in any of this. You never want to approach looking at your current beliefs from a place of judgment. You always want to look at them from a place of curiosity. As in, "isn't it interesting that I've been believing this?" Not, "I'm a bad person," or "I'm wrong," or "I've messed my whole life up by believing this." Judgment will only make you feel bad, and it's really not necessary. Your beliefs–regardless of how limiting they might be–have served you up to this point. And now you get to choose to let them go.

Change your beliefs from an empowering place, a place of possibility, not a place of judgment and ridicule.

Releasing Limiting Beliefs

The process for releasing limiting beliefs is pretty simple. First, decide that you're no longer available to believe that thing (whatever it is), and second, anytime that belief comes up, you remind yourself you're no longer believing that and shift yourself into thinking, saying, and believing the new belief instead.

You don't want to try and release old limiting beliefs without having something immediately available to replace them with. So, what I'd recommend is getting out a piece of paper or your journal, and on one side of the paper, write down the limiting beliefs you currently hold that go against you having what you want. And then on the opposite side of the paper, come up with a new belief you're going to replace the old one with. This is what's known as "crowding out."

I learned this concept when I was going through holistic health coaching school. The idea is instead of forcing yourself to stop eating the foods you don't want to be eating anymore (foods like sugar or dairy or gluten or whatever it might be for you), instead you start eating more of the good stuff. You eat more vegetables and fruit, along with the foods you don't want to be eating anymore.

As you do this, you'll begin to crowd out the old foods because you either won't want them anymore or you'll be so full from eating the good foods you won't be hungry for the ones you don't want to be eating. (And I'll add that I don't believe any food is good or bad; food is a neutral resource, like money. It's the meaning we give the food or money that makes us believe it's good or bad.)

This same crowding-out concept can be applied to releasing old beliefs and programming new ones. If you just continue to do your belief work every day, working with your subconscious mind to reprogram what's in there, you will eventually crowd out the old beliefs, to the point where you will either not believe them anymore, or when they pop up in your mind, you won't give them any weight or attention because they no longer feel true.

This is the work. But it doesn't have to be hard work. It might seem that way at first, but the more you do it, the more habitual it will become. Habits–whether actual physical habits or just ways of believing, thinking, and feeling–help you to thrive and make change a whole lot easier.

Quantum Leap Your Life: Chapter Two Recap

- **Commit to 1-2 times per day every day that you will work with your subconscious mind to change your beliefs (my recommendation is immediately upon waking and immediately before going to sleep)**–as a reminder, your subconscious mind controls everything you experience in your reality, and it's where your beliefs live. You must reprogram your subconscious mind to get a different result or experience in life. And your subconscious is reprogrammed through repetition, repetition, repetition.
- **Decide on your new beliefs**–once you've committed to set times in the day when you're going to work with your subconscious mind, choose the new beliefs you're going to program in. Stick with it and keep on going.
- **Release any old limiting beliefs**–get out a piece of paper or your journal, and on one side of the paper, write down the limiting beliefs you currently have that go against you having what you want. And then on

the opposite side of the paper, come up with a new
belief you're going to replace that old one with. Any
time those old beliefs resurface, stop what you're
doing, take a deep breath in and out, and then say to
yourself, "I choose to no longer believe that, and this is
what I am choosing to believe instead," and then
insert the new belief. Repeat this as often as you
need to.

Quantum Leap Your Life: Chapter Two Journal Prompts

For each of these prompts, do some freestyle journaling, or
answer in bullet points, whichever works best for you.

- What would I be believing if I made a quantum leap in
  the area(s) that I want to?
- What beliefs would someone have who already has
  the thing/the life that I want?
- What does belief mean to me?
- What would it look like for me today if I chose to
  believe that I was already at my next level in the
  area(s) I'm working on?

THREE

FEELING

The next part of quantum leaping is feeling the emotions that you'd be feeling if you were already the version of you who has what you want. The whole reason you want to be that version of yourself is because you believe it will feel a specific way to be that person and have those things. The problem with this is it puts those emotions–the ones you want to be feeling–off for a future time. But the truth is, you can feel whatever emotions you want to feel *right now*, and you don't need to be a different version of yourself for that to happen.

When you choose to feel those things now, instead of waiting to feel them later, you bring the future into the present. The more you do that, the more you feel like you're already that person, and that's when your physical reality starts to catch up. Making a quantum leap requires you to feel your feelings now.

The Feeling Is the Point

You've probably thought having the things you want is what will make you feel how you want to feel, but that's not true. Because when you get those things, they often won't feel the way you thought they would, and there will also be more things for you to want. Desire never dies. So rather than continue putting off feeling the way you want to feel, you can choose to feel it now. The feeling is the whole point of everything you want.

If I can convince you that the feelings are what you're actually after, not the things themselves, it will totally change your life. And yes, of course, you still get to have the things. But you have to start with the feelings.

What Feelings Would You Be Feeling?

So, what would you be feeling if you were the next-level version of yourself? If you had everything you want right now and more? Really dig into what those specific feelings would be for you.

And here's an example to help you out. Money is something that most people want to make a quantum leap in. They want to make and have more money. The question isn't, *how do I do that?* The question is, *what do I think (or believe) having the money I desire will do for me?*

I dug into that question a while back, and here's what came up for me. I believed that having the money I wanted would give me:

- Freedom
- The ability to say "No"
- Security
- Ease
- Peace of mind
- Infinite options

From this list, you can easily see that what I truly want isn't money, it's all of those things I listed. I thought I needed to have more money in order to experience those things. But the truth is, I can feel all of those emotions right now, without needing a single penny more than I currently have.

Now before you freak out, let me add that it's fine to want more money in your life. You're allowed to want it, you're allowed to have it, and you're worthy and deserving and good enough for it. You get to have money, and whatever else you want. Period.

So, yes, you might think you want a big house and a luxury car and ten vacations a year or whatever. And you may actually want those things. But dig deeper. What you really want, is the security you think that house will give you, or the fun and excitement of having that car, or the peace of mind and relaxation of those vacations.

So, what you really want on a deeper soul level is security, fun and excitement, peace of mind, and relaxation. Those are all things you can have right now. And if you choose to feel those feelings now, you will magnetize the things you want to you.

The Feeling Is the Path

This is the secret to having anything you want in your life, to being whoever you want to be, and to making a quantum leap any damn time you desire to. You must feel the feelings first. It's the path to getting to all of those things.

Using my same example from above of the things I believed I would feel by having more money, you can see that my path to making a quantum leap with money would be for me to find ways to feel all of those emotions right now. Those specific emotions are my path to money.

Now your path to money may be different. Since we all create our own realities, it's not about what *I* believe having more money will feel like. It's about what *you* believe it will feel like. And you may have very different feelings come up when you think about having more money (money is just an example, replace it with whatever it is you desire to have). So, your path to quantum leaping in any area of your life will be unique to you.

Answer this question for yourself: *what do I think having [insert what you want] will do for me?* You can also ask it this way: *what do I think being [insert who/how you want to be] will do for me?*

For example:

- What do I think having the love life I want will do for me?
- What do I think being fit and toned will do for me?
- What do I think having my dream house will do for me?
- What do I think being a famous author will do for me?
- What do I think having a luxury car will do for me?
- What do I think being rich will do for me?

This is what you have to dig into and get clear on. The things you want are just the surface level. It's time to go deeper and connect with your answer on a soul level.

How To Feel Those Things Now

You're probably thinking, *"Okay, fine, I get it, what I really want is the deeper things, not the surface things, but how do I feel those feelings now before I have the surface-level stuff?"* This is something I've spent years figuring out for myself. I now consider myself an expert in creating specific emotional states (what a weird thing to be an expert in, ha-ha).

There are three main ways to create a specific emotional state:

- Determine what in your life already makes you feel that emotion
- Figure out what else you could bring into your life that would make you feel that emotion
- Visualize

Continuing on with my money example and the things I believed I would feel as a result of having it, I can take each one of those emotions and dig into what feeling that emotion right now might look like for me.

Let's take *peace of mind* and then apply it to the three main ways to create a specific emotional state. You can use this same process with any emotional states you want to create for yourself.

Here's what creating peace of mind could look like for me:

1. Determine what in your life already makes you feel peace of mind

First, I would look for all of the things, places, people, activities, etc., in my life that cause me to feel peace of mind. Some things I can think of are:

- My bedroom closet–it's so neat and clean and organized
- Putting all of my bills on auto payment–this allows me to make sure everything gets paid on time
- Freestyle journaling–to get out whatever noise is in my head at that moment
- Meditation–to calm the inner chaos

Since these things are already in my life and make me feel peace of mind, I would focus on how I could spend more time being involved in those things. For example, there are some days when I'll just stand in my bedroom closet and stare at everything for ten to fifteen minutes. My boyfriend always laughs at me when I do this, but I love the peace I feel when I'm in that closet.

2. Figure out what else you could bring into your life that makes you feel peace of mind

Secondly, I would look for all of the things, places, people, activities, etc., in general, that cause me to feel peace of mind, and see how I could bring more of them into my life. Some things I can think of are:

- Organization–I love the idea of having a home where every room is neat and organized with a specific place for everything
- Making crafts–this is something I've loved since I was a kid and have done on and off as an adult
- Automation–not having to think about things, like scheduling appointments or paying bills, but just having them taken care of automatically

Now I have some options for additional ways I can create and feel peace of mind in my daily life. I could automate more of my bills if I have any that aren't on auto payment. I could spend more time making crafts or building things in my dad's workshop, which are two things that bring me so much peace and joy. And I could spend time organizing every room in my house, so they all give me the same feeling that my bedroom closet does.

3. Visualize

Lastly, is to visualize the things you want as if you already have them now, and bring in the emotions you'd be feeling as you do that. With *peace of mind* as the example, I could visualize things like:

- Me sitting on a beach with my feet up, a book in my hands, and not a worry in the world

- Me looking at my bills for the month and every single one of them is paid in full already
- Me laying on my bed, watching my dog fast asleep next to me

The idea is to match the visual with the emotion you want to experience. This is how you can bring a specific emotion into your internal experience.

But I will add that, for me, visualization is less about bringing in a specific emotion, and more about visualizing myself already having the outcome I want or already having made the quantum leap. As I visualize myself already there, the emotions I'd be experiencing automatically start coming up for me. Most days, I bring myself to happy tears while I'm visualizing because it feels so real to me as I'm seeing it in my mind.

I've had a visualization practice for years, so don't beat yourself up if you're not able to feel the emotions right away. Something that helped me many years ago when I was first starting to visualize and feel the emotions inside myself was to start by imagining something I already had that I felt grateful for. Nine times out of ten, that meant I was visualizing my dog. Once I could feel the emotions heightening inside my body, then I would start to cut in images of the things that I desired to have.

Your brain can't decipher whether what it's imagining is real or not. So, by mixing images of things you already have that you're grateful for with images of things you desire to have, it causes your subconscious mind to start associating the things you want with the feeling of already having them.

A more advanced technique for visualizing is to not just see yourself in the picture, like you're watching a movie, but to visualize from your own perspective. So you would visualize what you'd be seeing from your vantage point as you imagine the life you want. For example, you'd see your hands wrapped around the steering wheel of your dream car, rather than just imagining yourself owning the car. This can help create the feelings of having it now even more.

And if you have a hard time seeing images when you visualize, you can do a couple of different things to help yourself out:

- Look up specific images that represent the thing(s) you want, and then when you're visualizing, imagine those images that you looked up, rather than trying to create the images with your mind
- Write out your visualization like you're telling a story, and include as many of your senses in the description as possible; this will help you to feel it, even if you can't see it with images in your mind

Struggling with the Specific Emotions

If you're having a hard time naming the specific emotions you'd feel as your quantum-leaped self, or if you just can't figure out how to match those specific feelings, you can default to just feeling good. Feeling good is enough. Feeling good will put you on the path to everything you desire to be, do and have.

And you would still use those same three applications we discussed in the section above–determining what in your life already makes you feel good, figuring out what else would feel good to you that you can bring into your life, and visualizing feeling good–to create feel-good emotions in your body and mind.

I find focusing on feeling good to be an easy default for when you're not clear on the specific emotions, or just don't know what would make you feel the way you want to feel. I used a focus on feeling good, in general, to change my entire life back in 2018-2019, when I manifested a divorce from an unaligned marriage, and then manifested the love of my life not long after that (you can read more about how I did this in my book, *F*ck the How*). I didn't know the specific emotions I'd be feeling if I had the love and relationship I wanted, so I just did whatever I could to feel good, in general, every day. And that was enough to quantum leap me from living the wrong life to living the life I knew I was meant for.

The Feel-Good List

The feel-good list is my go-to tool for tapping into the emotional state of feeling good. How it works is, you make a list of everything you can think of that makes you feel good. It can literally be anything. Here's some of what's on my list:

- Writing
- Making videos and audios (for TikTok, YouTube, and/or my podcast)
- Getting a massage
- Taking a nap
- Watching a movie (usually a rom-com)
- Walking my dog
- Being by the water (which usually means going to the lake)
- The color blue
- Getting my nails done
- Wearing rings
- Reading books and magazines
- Cooking and baking
- Dancing
- Yoga and/or working out
- Driving in my Jeep
- Listening to music

I think you get the idea. When I come across something new in my life that feels good to me, I add it to the list. And then whenever I want to shift my emotional state, I pull out my list, choose one or more things off of it and go do them. So, I might wear something blue and then drive in my Jeep while listening to music on the way to get my nails done. And I'll feel good the whole time.

I talk about the feel-good list in a lot of my books, and that's because it works. It's a super helpful way to shift your emotional state anytime you want to. I can't rave about it enough. So, make your list and keep it close by, in your journal or on your phone (which is where I keep mine). That doesn't mean you ever have to use it, but it's there when you want it or when you need a quick mood-booster.

Your Feel-Good Phrase

Another tool that's really useful to have in your arsenal is the feel-good phrase. This is a phrase that, when you say it to yourself, makes you feel really good. This could also be called an affirmation, but I don't like calling it that because affirmations don't work unless they create an emotional charge for you.

Your phrase can be anything that feels good to you, and you may have to test out different phrases and tweak the wording until you can really feel it. Here's an example of one of my feel-good phrases and how I tweaked it until I felt an emotional charge.

There's an author and coach I follow online who is known for the phrase: *My work is of high service and worthy of massive compensation.* I love this phrase and have tried using it for years in my own life. But the problem I always ran into was that it never felt good to me. No matter how many times I said it, the phrase just didn't create any emotions for me. Until recently, when I decided to change the words "my work" to "my books." Now the phrase I use is: *My books are of high service and worthy of massive compensation.* When I say that phrase, it creates an emotional charge in me. I feel it on a deep soul level. It gives me chills to say it out loud because I believe it so much.

Start with a phrase that you would like to use. Say it out loud a few times to see how it feels to you. Tweak the wording until you can really feel it inside of you. Then commit to using that phrase anytime you need a quick mood-shifter. Repeat as often as you need to. You can have as many feel-good phrases as you want. Either memorize the phrases or write them down somewhere you can keep them close to you, like on your phone.

What If It's Not an Emotion?

You may be wondering—what about the things that are scenarios rather than emotions? After all, you can't very well feel "the ability to say No," as in my example about how I'd feel when I had more money. But scenarios still have an emotional tie-in if you dig a little deeper.

Having more money would allow me the ability to say no whenever I wanted to. But what would the ability to say no do for me? It would create more freedom, it would allow me to make space for the things that truly lit me up, and it would bring me joy to not have to do things I didn't want to do. From this, you can see that free, lit up, and joy, are all emotional states. And that's what I would focus on creating for myself.

The same goes for any non-emotion scenarios that come up for you when you think about having what you want. If you dig below the surface, you'll be able to come up with emotions that would tie in, and you can then choose to feel those as well.

What's the Point of All of This?

The point of dealing with the emotions, and feeling the feelings you would be experiencing when you make your quantum leap is to start becoming that version of yourself now, through your emotional state. When you feel different, you start to make different choices and decisions, take different actions, and become more like the version of you who has what you want. It just starts to happen automatically as you feel more like that person.

An example I have of this is when I wanted to become a consistent exerciser. I started first with the mindset and programmed in the beliefs that I was a fit person, that exercise was easy for me, and that I was consistent with my fitness. Then I started to feel the emotions of being that version of me. I felt the emotions of gratitude for my body, and joy and appreciation for all it does for me. And in doing that, I began a daily fitness practice, which didn't take as much effort as I thought it would because I was already feeling like the version of me who had a habit around this. I created the habit almost immediately, and on the days when I didn't want to work out, I would still do it anyhow because I knew that's what the fit version of me would choose to do. By creating the mindset and emotional state first, I was able to step into the actions with ease and make different choices and decisions along with it. And I've kept this up for years because I not only feel like a fit person who has a habit of exercising, but I actually *am* that person now.

Stop Feeling Lack

One of the worst feelings is the feeling of lack. A lot of times, we feel lack when we don't have the things that we want, and that's actually the reason we don't end up getting them. Lack creates more lack. So, more than anything else, you have to figure out how to stop yourself from feeling lack.

This isn't about never feeling bad. You're human, and negative emotions are a part of life. Don't try to bypass your emotions. If quantum leaping required you to feel good all the time, then you wouldn't be able to receive a windfall of money when someone dies and leaves it to you. But that happens all the time for people. They're sad, and yet they still receive money.

So, this is simply about removing the feeling of lack, as much as you possibly can. And you do that by applying all of the things we've talked about in this chapter. The more you feel the next-level you emotions, the less lack you'll feel.

Quantum Leap Your Life: Chapter Three Recap

- **What would you be feeling if you were the next-level version of yourself?**–figure out the specific emotions you would be feeling when you make your quantum leap, and then start creating those emotional states for yourself right now.
- **Determine what in your life already makes you feel those emotions (or just makes you feel good, in general)**–start by determining where in your life you're already feeling those "next-level you" emotions, and spend more time doing those things.
- **Figure out what else would make you feel those emotions (or just feel good, in general) that you can bring into your life right now**–look at how else you could feel those "next-level you" emotions, and bring some of that stuff into your life right now.
- **Create your feel-good list**–make a list of everything that feels good to you. It doesn't matter what it is. If it feels good to you, it goes on the list. And then whenever you want to feel good or shift your mood, pick something off that list and go do it.
- **Come up with your feel-good phrase**–create your feel-good phrase, so you can have it on hand to use whenever you want to shift your mood in the moment. Create multiples phrases if that feels good to you, one for each area you want to make a quantum leap in.

Quantum Leap Your Life: Chapter Three Journal Prompts

For each of these prompts, do some freestyle journaling, or answer in bullet points, whichever works best for you.

- How would I feel if I were to make a quantum leap in the area(s) I want to?
- What does feeling good mean to me?
- What would feeling good look like for me today?

FOUR
THINKING

We have more than six-thousand thoughts every single day, according to a Healthline.com article based on a 2020 study of brain thought patterns, conducted by Nature Communications, a highly respected peer-reviewed journal (https://www.healthline.com/health/how-many-thoughts-per-day#thoughts-per-day). These thoughts are a mix of things like musings, deep inquisitions, observations, and patterns. And because we have so many thoughts, it can be hard to monitor and manage all of them.

But if you want to make a quantum leap, changing your thoughts is also a part of it. You have to be thinking the thoughts the next-level version of you would be thinking, not staying stuck in your current thought patterns. So, the more awareness you can cultivate around your thoughts–what you're thinking, whether those thoughts are aligned with who you want to be, and what you desire to have–the better.

Awareness is a gift. When you're aware, you can catch yourself and make a change. When you're operating unconsciously with no awareness of the thoughts that are running through your mind, you can't do that.

It's about your in-the-moment thinking, and being willing to look at it and make a change when it doesn't match how your quantum-leaped self would be thinking. Most importantly, you have to be aware of your thought patterns.

Thought Patterns

A thought pattern is a thought or set of thoughts you continue to think over and over again. You often find yourself thinking these same things every day, sometimes all day, every day. That's a pattern. It's something repetitive that keeps happening.

It's unfortunate, but for most of us, our patterned ways of thinking are negative. We've been programmed to think this way, based on things like what we were taught growing up, what we observed early on in our lives, societal beliefs, and what the people around us are saying. And it's these negative patterns that you need to be aware of and committed to breaking.

An easy way to find your thought patterns is to ask yourself: *what do I find myself thinking about a lot of the time?* What are the specific thoughts or types of thoughts that you notice yourself having most of the time?

Some examples could be:

- I'm not there yet
- It's not working
- This is too hard
- Life is against me

A thought pattern isn't always negative. You can also have positive thought patterns. If a thought makes you feel good, it's a positive thought. If it makes you feel bad, it's a negative one. You can use your feelings as guidance on what type of thought patterns you're encountering.

Thought Pattern Triggers

Everyone is triggered by something, and when those triggers happen, they usually lead to thinking a whole bunch of negative thoughts that don't serve you. When you can be clear and aware of what specifically triggers your negative thought patterns, you can then put provisions in place to deal with them.

In my life, something that used to trigger negative thoughts for me was when I didn't make any money in my online business for a whole week. When this occurred, I would go down a negative thought spiral, thinking things like, *"This isn't working, why am I not there yet? Why does this keep happening? When are things finally going to change for me? I'm just as good as all those other online entrepreneurs, so why am I not making money like they are?"* None of those thoughts were helpful. They didn't make me feel good, and they definitely didn't help me to be–or think like–the quantum-leaped version of me.

Once I was clear on this trigger–not making money in my online business for a week–I was able to put a provision in place to help offset the negative thoughts. A provision is a plan you put in place to handle any liabilities that might happen. Negative thought patterns are liabilities because they get in the way of you thinking how you want to think and being who you want to be.

The provision I put in place was that if I had a week where I didn't make any money in my online business, I would instead look at all of the other ways I *did* make money that week. My online business is not my only source of income. I have multiple sources of income, including my books, which are my favorite income source. So, if I had a week where no money came in through my online business, instead of going down a negative thought spiral, I would log into my Amazon KDP account (for self-published authors), and I would look at all of the book sales I made that week. Seeing that I actually did make money always made me feel better, which stopped the negative thoughts in their tracks.

Here are some more examples of negative thought pattern triggers and provisions you could put in place:

Trigger: Seeing someone on social media bragging about how much money their business made that month
Provision: Unfollow the people who trigger you

Trigger: A family member constantly tells you your dreams are unrealistic and not going to happen
Provision: Stop talking to that person about your dreams

Trigger: Seeing bad news being posted on social media when you first wake up in the morning
Provision: Stop checking social media until later in the day, after you've done your mindset practice and are feeling mentally stronger/better able to handle it

Your mindset is one of the most important tools you have when making a quantum leap, so do whatever is required for you to protect it.

What Thoughts Do I Want to Be Thinking?

With over six-thousand thoughts going through your head every day, mostly unconsciously, you'll want to spend some time considering which specific thoughts or types of thoughts you want to be thinking. Most importantly, you'll want to consider which thoughts your quantum-leaped self would be thinking.

That's not to say that you won't still have negative thoughts. But at that level, you'll be more practiced in not allowing yourself to entertain those thoughts. When negative thoughts come across your mind, you'll recognize them for what they are—because you've got the awareness that you didn't have before making the leap—and you'll be more able to let them go.

So, what thoughts do you want to be thinking? What do you want your mind to be occupied with the majority of the time? I try to spend the majority of my time consciously thinking about who I want to be and where I want to go in my life, as well as repeating my belief statements over and over again as often as I can remember.

Daydreaming is a great tool for gaining better control of your thoughts. I know you've probably been taught that daydreaming is nonsense, a waste of time, and delusional, but it's not. Daydreaming allows you to keep the things you desire to have, do and be in the front of your mind. And it saves you from constantly playing out potential negative scenarios and situations or looking back at past pains, which just keeps them in your current reality.

You need to go past your current "what is" and allow yourself to imagine what can and will be. Daydreaming is great for that. So, give yourself permission to daydream anytime you want to, as long as it feels good to you (if it doesn't, it's not going to help).

A common question I get asked by clients and my online community is: *what about intrusive negative thoughts? What do I do when I catch myself thinking negatively?* And for that, I use and recommend the Stop-and-Swap Method.

The Stop-and-Swap Method

This is a method I created for myself when I was in the process of quantum leaping my love life. I would very often catch myself worrying that I'd never get to have the relationship I wanted, and I had fearful thoughts about being stuck in the marriage I was in forever. I knew thoughts like that were not going to help me quantum leap in my love life, so I had to put a stop to them as soon as I caught myself thinking that way.

What I implemented is a method I now call the Stop-and-Swap. Here's how it works:

1. You're going along through your day and you catch yourself thinking negatively, worrying, and/or going down a negative thought spiral.
2. You say to yourself, out loud if possible, "STOP!" The "STOP" is a pattern interrupt that stops your thoughts in that moment.
3. Remind yourself that's not how you want to be thinking, and that kind of thinking won't help you make your quantum leap.
4. Ask yourself: *what can I think instead?*
5. Swap the thoughts you were thinking for new, positive ones that align with you being who you want to be and having what you want to have.

And here's a specific example to help illustrate this:

1. You're washing dishes and you're worrying about how you're going to make your dream happen. You're thinking things like, *it's never going to happen for me, I'm too old, it's just too late, I don't come from that kind of family anyhow, it's taking too long, I'm never going to have what I want, etc.*
2. As soon as you notice this is happening, you immediately say, "STOP!" Now you've interrupted the negative thought spiral.
3. You then remind yourself that thinking about those things isn't helping you, and you decide in the moment you don't want to be thinking that way anymore. Your decision is powerful.
4. You ask yourself, "*what can I think instead?*" And some better-feeling thoughts that occur to you include: *there are plenty of people who weren't successful until their later*

years and I can be one of them too, it's not my job to figure out the how, the Universe is working with me to co-create my dream, I'm getting closer and closer every day, etc.

5. Now you're going to swap those new thoughts in and allow yourself to spend a few minutes going down that positive thought spiral.
6. Repeat as often as you need to.

Awareness and commitment are what make the Stop-and-Swap work. You have to be committed to shifting your thoughts as soon as you catch yourself thinking negatively.

If you touch a hot burner on your stove, you know it's going to burn you, so you intentionally do your best to never do that. What if you did the same thing with negative thoughts? What if you intentionally decided not to indulge in them because you know you'll just get burned?

No longer give yourself permission to wallow in the thoughts you don't want to be thinking. This takes practice, but it's also just a decision you make. *I will not think like that anymore. I will not allow myself to indulge in my negative thoughts. I will assume every negative thought about myself is a lie and I will not entertain it.*

When you catch yourself thinking negatively, making a huge thought shift in that moment probably won't happen. But you can always find a better-feeling thought. No matter what you're thinking, there is always a thought that would feel even slightly better. Commit yourself to shifting to that better-feeling thought as soon as you're aware that you're thinking in ways that aren't helpful to your quantum leap.

This method isn't about getting rid of your negative thoughts so you never have them again. You're always going to have some negative thoughts pop up from time to time. It's about being fully committed to self-awareness and not letting yourself go down that negative thought spiral.

And whatever you do, don't let the negative thoughts, or the fact that you were thinking them, mean anything.

You Create the Meaning

Something I learned when I was going through the *Landmark Forum* (a personal development workshop) is that humans are meaning-making machines. We just love to make meaning out of everything. It's what helps us to relate to the people and the world around us. But what I also learned from studying *A Course in Miracles* with my friend (who is a reverend) over the last year, is that nothing has any meaning except for the meaning we choose to give it.

If you don't make your negative thoughts mean anything, then they won't. But most of the time, you've given them a lot of weight, and you've made them mean things like:

- You're not good enough
- You don't get to have what you want
- You'll never make a change in your life
- Quantum leaping is for other people but not for you

And that's all nonsense. You having negative thoughts doesn't mean any of those things. They're just negative thoughts, and they can't impact you unless you decide to let them.

At this point in my life journey, I have made peace with the fact that I will always have negative thoughts. It's just a part of being human, but they don't mean anything about me or my life or my future. I'm the one who gets to decide, and I've chosen to see negative thoughts as meaningless lies that I won't give any weight to.

And you can do the same.

A Perspective Shift

Your perspective on yourself, your life, and your current reality matters because it creates what you experience in your day-to-day life. If you think of yourself in a certain way, you will always see yourself that way and you will experience things that line up with that perspective. That doesn't mean it's the only option available, it's just the one you've chosen up to this point.

For example, I got bullied from a very early age. When I was five years old, my cousins who were a couple of years older than me, used to pick on me, call me names, and make fun of me. That bullying then followed me into my school years. I got bullied by kids at my morning latchkey program. I got bullied on the school bus. I got bullied in the hallway at school between classes. This happened over and over and over again for all of the years I was in school.

I had a perspective that I was a victim who always got bullied. And this perspective of myself continued to show up in my life because that is how I thought of myself. I also had several other traumatizing situations happen which kept me feeling like a victim in my life.

But all of this happened because that is how I saw myself. If I had changed my perspective, I would've gotten a different result. And I did change it, as soon as I went to college.

In college, I decided to think of myself differently. I chose a college that was two and a half hours away from where I grew up. No one at my college knew me or knew what I went through previously. I had the opportunity to let all of that go and think of myself in a different way. So that's what I did.

I decided I got to have popular friends and be a popular, well-liked student. And that became my college experience.

I was well-known and well-liked by my classmates and the professors. I had loads of friends. I was invited to all kinds of parties and gatherings and groups. And I never got bullied ever again. By changing my perspective of myself and how I saw and thought about myself, I changed my entire experience of life.

This works with anything in any area of your life. So, consider how you've been thinking about, viewing, and/or perceiving yourself, specific areas of your life, the world, etc., up until now. And then decide how you want to think about, view, and perceive those things. Changing your perception, especially about the area(s) you want to make a quantum leap in, is super important.

The Daily Mindset Practice

Something that will help you to shift your perspective and tame your negative thoughts is having a daily mindset practice. A mindset practice is a set of specific actions or activities that you do to work on cultivating the mindset you desire to have every day. I've been doing a daily mindset practice since August 2015 when I was first introduced to this idea, and I've kept it up ever since. I've changed the activities within my practice many times over the years, but I've never veered away from doing something every day to work on my mindset.

Mental strength is a lot like muscle strength. The more you work it, the stronger it gets. Weak thinking comes from living unconsciously and not being aware that your thoughts matter. Your thoughts do matter, and they matter a lot, especially if you want to make a quantum leap.

The reason I recommend doing a daily practice is that it's easier to do something every day and make a habit of it than it is to do it sporadically. And this doesn't have to be something that takes you a ton of time. You can do a mindset practice in ten minutes. I originally started working on my mindset every day for five to ten minutes, and then I increased the time as I went along and realized how much it was helping me.

There are three parts to a mindset practice that I feel are important:

1. **Clear**–you have to clear out the noise and clutter going on in your mind before you can program anything new in there
2. **Reset to truth**–remind yourself and reprogram in the truths that you now choose to think and believe

3. **Feel it**–connect those beliefs and thoughts with an emotional state

There are a lot of different ways that you can do these three things. But for the sake of just getting started and keeping it up, I'm going to share with you the specific practice I recommend. If you want to learn more about different options for each of these three parts, check out my book, *F*ck the How*, where I talk more in depth about each part.

Here's the practice that I recommend starting off with. Once you get this one down, you can change up how you're doing it to include more of what you prefer. There are no rules, just guidelines, and then finding what works best for you. This only takes ten minutes to do, but feel free to take longer if you want to.

First, you're going to get out a journal or notebook and you're going to write stream-of-consciousness for at least one page (but feel free to do more). Stream-of-consciousness means you're just writing down whatever comes out, and it can literally be anything. You can write about the thoughts you're having in the moment. You can complain about things that are bothering you. You can make a grocery list. Whatever comes up, comes out. No judgments. Just write it down and fill at least one page.

Doing this type of journaling gets the crap out of your head. Putting it onto paper actually releases it from your mind, allowing you to think clearer, and be more connected to your thoughts. It also unblocks you so the good stuff can come through (things like inspired ideas, actions you can take, creative projects, etc.).

Next, you're going to write out your desired reality. This can be done in a couple of different ways–you can write it out like it's a journal entry of something that has already happened, or you can write out specific belief statements and positive things that you want to be thinking. Keep it focused on the area you want to make a quantum leap in. Do this for at least one page.

(Refer back to your new beliefs from Chapter Two if you're not sure what to write.)

Finally, you're going to go back through every statement you just wrote down, and you're going to read through it, taking a moment to pause at each belief statement and repeat it a few times before moving on to the next one. As you're repeating each statement, feel into it actually being true for you right now. Create the feeling inside of yourself as you read it.

No matter what you do every day, if you commit to working on your mindset, it will change your life.

Quantum Leap Your Life: Chapter Four Recap

- **What are your current thought patterns? What thoughts do you catch yourself thinking over and over again?**–get clear on this, and then write it down so you can maintain awareness.
- **What are the things that trigger those thought patterns?**–when you know the trigger, you can put a provision in place to support you.
- **What provision(s) can you put in place to counteract the thought-pattern triggers?**–make a list of the things that trigger you and then the provisions you're putting in place for each one. Keep it close to you so that when you find yourself getting triggered, you can use the appropriate provision to defuse it immediately.
- **What thoughts do you want to be thinking?**–where do you want your thoughts to go most of the day? Which topics, perspectives, memories, or positive thoughts do you want to be focused on? Make a list so you have some awareness around potential thoughts you can "Stop and Swap" to when the negative ones pop up.

- **What have you given false meaning to?**–consider especially the area(s) you want to make a quantum leap in and any unsupportive meaning you've given to anything in that area. Then remind yourself that nothing means anything except the meaning you give it, and give those things a different meaning.
- **Create a daily mindset practice for yourself, or use the one I suggested above, and commit to doing it every day for at least 10 minutes from here on out**– this is the one thing that will truly begin to change the way you think.

Quantum Leap Your Life: **Chapter Four Journal Prompts**

For each of these prompts, do some freestyle journaling, or answer in bullet points, whichever works best for you.

- How would I be thinking if I had already made a quantum leap in the area(s) that I want to?
- How would the version of me who's already "there" be thinking?
- What thoughts would the version of me who already has the things I want be thinking?
- What would someone who already has what I want be thinking?

FIVE

ACTING AS IF

I'm the most excited about this chapter. Not only because teaching you how to act as if is one of my favorite things ever, but also because your acting as if actions can actually override any limiting and negative thoughts, beliefs and feelings you may still have going on. Acting as if actions are a powerful way to show the Universe that you believe you get to be the person you want to be and have the things you want to have. And that acting in faith of receiving, as I like to call it, can move mountains *fast*.

We've talked so far about believing, feeling, and thinking like the version of you who has made a quantum leap in the area(s) you want to make one in. Acting as if is putting actions behind all of those beliefs, feelings, and thoughts. Because if you were already the version of you who had made a quantum leap, there are actions you would be taking. There are things you'd be doing in your physical reality to ready yourself, and to prepare the way.

So first, what does it mean to act as if with your actions? It means you take action like the version of you who has the thing that you want and who is the person you desire to be.

That version of you already exists as a possibility. Now you just have to choose her (or him) and keep on choosing. That person is already inside of you. You just have to pull her (or him) out. And you do that through changing your beliefs, shifting your thoughts, creating the emotional state that matches, and then acting as if.

Acting In Faith of Receiving

Acting as if is where shit starts to get real. This is the part that most people stop at because it's scary to put yourself out there, to show with your actions that you believe, and to risk something, even in a small way. That's why I like to see acting as if as acting in faith of receiving. You're not just taking random actions and hoping they work. You're believing that you are the person who gets to have the things you want, and then you're backing that belief up with action. You're *demonstrating your faith through action*. And that's huge. Even if the actions you take are baby steps. The size of the action isn't really what matters. It's that the action is aligned with you making a quantum leap.

Acting as if requires a level of trust and faith. Trust that you do get to have what you want. Trust that the Universe is working on your behalf. Trust that it's all going to work out. And faith that if you take action and trust the process, you will be greatly rewarded in your physical reality. You're no longer just thinking, feeling, and believing for your next level. You're taking action with faith that all of those thoughts, beliefs, and feelings are and will eventually be true.

What Would You Be Doing?

The simplest thing to start with is to consider what actions you would be taking if you were the person who already had the thing(s) that you want. That version of you is different than who you are right now (otherwise you would already have what you want.) By doing more of the things you would be doing if you were already "there," you close the gap and bring the "there" into the now. And you want to hit this from every angle possible. Not because you have to do or implement every action you come up with, but because you want to have a complete look at who you would be as that version of you.

Here are some things to start with. If you were already that person who has the thing(s) that you want...

- What habits would you have in place?
- What would your day-to-day life be like?
- How would you be spending your time every day?
- How would you be showing up in your life? In your relationships? In your business and/or career? In your health and fitness?
- What would you be eating?
- What would you be wearing?
- What decisions or choices would you be making that you're not making right now?

Once you're clear on the stuff I just listed, you can begin to implement some of it in your life right now, as if you're already that person.

For example, one of the areas I was working on quantum leaping in was my body. I had desired a certain body type for a long time, and I was close to having it, but I wasn't putting in the work to fully claim it for myself. So, I decided to act as if my way into having that body, starting with my clothing.

I recently did a major closet clean-out and reorganization. I was feeling stuck in the area of clothing and sick of everything in my closet. I knew the quantum-leaped version of me wouldn't be wearing most of what was in there. The old me hid her body and wore baggy, oversized t-shirts and sweatpants. But the me who had made a quantum leap in her physical body and health would dress differently. I would be wearing a lot of crop tops–which are one of my favorite things–because I'd be happy with and proud of the body I created for myself. I would wear fitted clothing. I would mostly wear jeans. I would have a refined, classic style that I could easily mix trendy pieces into.

I had recently learned about the idea of creating a "classic capsule" from a company called Glow Fashion. The concept is so simple and yet brilliant. You build your entire closet around twelve classic wardrobe staples that never go out of style (things like jeans, a white button-up blouse, neutral t-shirts, a blazer, black pants, a motorcycle jacket, etc). When I heard about this concept, I knew right away that next-level me would have a wardrobe like this.

So, I decided to totally revamp my closet around this concept. I first went through and pulled out all of the capsule pieces I already owned and put them into their own section of the closet. Then I tried on everything else in my closet to see what I wanted to keep and what I wanted to get rid of. I ended up with three bags full of clothes that I no longer wanted, that did not feel like next-level me. I kept only the capsule items, plus the personality pieces (basically anything else in your wardrobe that's not part of the capsule) that felt like next-level me. Now getting dressed every day is so easy, and I love everything in my closet.

Doing this closet clean-out and reorganization was me acting as if I was already the version of me who made a quantum leap in my physical body and health. My old closet represented who I was, my new closet represents who I desire to be. I closed the gap between the old me and the new me by changing what I was wearing. And now when I put those clothes on, I feel like a different version of myself. I feel more mature and refined and stylish, just like I know my quantum-leaped self would feel. I didn't wait until I became that version of myself to clean out my closet and create my capsule wardrobe. I did it now, knowing full well where I'm headed and who I'm choosing to be.

The mistake many people make is choosing to wait. They wait for the thing they want to show up. They wait for the new job, the new relationship, the money, the whatever before they make any changes to their lives and their actions. And this is actually what keeps them waiting. Because they're not taking any action. They're not putting any "skin in the game," which just means being willing to risk something in pursuit of becoming who they want to be and having what they want to have.

Yes, it might seem risky to get rid of so much stuff in my closet and build a closet around becoming another version of myself. What if it doesn't happen? What if I never become that person? What if I never have that body? Then I won't have any of the clothes I used to wear. But the truth is, it has to happen when you take action like it's already done. It might take some time, but if you just keep taking action and acting as if you're already there, you will be there before you know it.

One of the biggest reasons I held off for so long on cleaning out my closet and creating the capsule wardrobe and wearing what I wanted to be wearing was because I "didn't yet have the body I wanted." I kept telling myself I would revamp my closet and wear what I wanted to when I had my desired physical body. But doing that was keeping it away from me. It was keeping me from doing anything about having that body. Allowing myself to hide in sweatpants and baggy tees kept me not exercising consistently or doing what it took to have the physical body I desired.

But once I removed all that stuff and only had a closet full of clothes I'd be wearing if I already had that body, it forced me to take action on actually creating it for myself. Today, I have a consistent habit of exercising five to six days a week. I'm eating healthier than ever before. I feel more comfortable in my own skin, I'm happily able to dress how I want to, and I have the physical body I've always desired. My dream physical body was created by acting as if I already had it before I actually did.

Another example would be my writing career, which is another area I'm working on quantum leaping in. Something I've wanted since I was eleven years old is to see my fictional stories turned into movies. I write a lot of nonfiction books, but my true love always has been fictional storytelling. I've written a few novels, and over the past few years, I've gotten more into screenwriting. I've written four screenplays, and have loads of ideas for more I could write. Being a Hollywood screenwriter is definitely something I see in the vision for my dream writing career.

So, I could apply this same acting as if concept to being a Hollywood screenwriter. I would first ask myself, *if I was already a Hollywood screenwriter, what would be true for me?* And here's what came up for me when I asked that question just now. I would...

- Have a membership to Stage32 (a social networking site for people in the Hollywood industry)
- Be connecting with and networking with people in the industry on a regular basis
- Write more screenplays, so I have a large catalog of work to pull from
- Enter my screenplays in more contests, which is a great way to show off my work and get connected with people in the industry
- Meet with industry executives who I can show my work to and get feedback from
- Have a daily habit of consistently working on my screenplays
- Continually be developing new story ideas to be written into screenplays

Just from this list, you can already see a bunch of actions I could take to close the gap between where I am now and becoming the Hollywood screenwriter I desire to be.

But knowing what actions you could take is only half the battle. The other half is actually taking those actions. It's giving yourself permission to act as if what you want is already yours, in whichever ways you can right now.

And like I said before, the actions don't have to be big actions. If you want to make a quantum leap in your money situation, for example, you could take a massive action, like hiring a financial planner or a money coach. Or you could do something smaller like buying yourself a nicer wallet, one that makes you feel good to keep your money in. The version of you who has more money would most definitely have a nice wallet, so that's an acting as if action you can easily take. The smaller actions will add up. When you take one action in the direction of your dreams, the Universe more than matches your efforts.

You have to figure out which actions would feel best to you. The feeling is what you're after. If an action doesn't feel good, it's probably not the right action for you. Some actions may be intimidating, but that doesn't make them bad actions to take. You have to check in with yourself to see if you would feel good having taken that action.

For example, it's very intimidating for me to think about meeting with industry executives and showing them my screenplays, but I know afterward I would feel really good about having taken that action. That's how I know it's the right action for me to take.

What's cool is, when you begin taking the act as if actions you can think of right now, you'll also receive inspired actions. An inspired action is an idea for an action you can take or something you can do, say, etc., that just pops into your head or that is inspired by something you hear or see. These are the actions that are the most powerful because they're literally the Universe sending you the "how" for becoming who you want to be and having what you want to have. If you commit to always taking the inspired actions, even when they don't seem to make logical sense, you'll be amazed by how fast you get to where you want to be.

Prepare To Receive

Another way of looking at this is, how can you prepare to receive your quantum leap? How can you prepare yourself and your life to make this leap? Preparation of any kind signals to the Universe that you're ready to receive. That you can handle it because you've prepared yourself.

The metaphor I like to use to explain this is a frozen pizza. If you decide to eat a frozen pizza for dinner and then you remove that pizza from the freezer and pop it into a hot oven, you know at some point, your pizza will be cooked and ready to eat. You don't put the pizza into the oven and then worry that it might not cook. You don't come up with another option for dinner, just in case the pizza doesn't work out. You don't decide after a few minutes that it's "not working" and go do something else for dinner instead.

You simply prepare to eat the pizza. You get out your dishes. You set your table. You pour your favorite beverage. Maybe you figure out what movie you're going to watch if you like to watch movies while you eat. You get ready, and you prepare yourself to eat that pizza when it's done cooking.

The same goes for your quantum leap. If you know what you want and you believe you get to have it, then it's just a matter of preparing the way however you can. It will be different for every person and every quantum leap, but there are always preparatory actions you can take.

For example, if you want to make a quantum leap into a whole new career, you can prepare the way by:

- Figuring out what kind of career you'd like to have
- Researching which options are available in your area and/or what's required for you to move into that type of job
- Starting to apply for jobs
- Updating your resume

- Signing up for classes or courses that will teach you any new skills you may need to do the new job
- Meeting with someone who has that job or career and ask them any questions you may have about it
- Starting to get into a flow of the new job–if you haven't been working, for example, start getting up at the time you'd need to get up for that job
- Buying yourself a new lunch bag
- Cleaning up and clearing out your desk at your current job of all your personal items, so you're ready at a moment's notice to hop into your new job

These are just examples, and you have to do what feels like preparation for you.

When I wanted to make a quantum leap from having a day job to working for myself, I prepared the way by doing a handful of the things I just listed:

- I signed up for a six-month business building workshop
- I created several offers to sell in my business
- I made connections with people who I wanted to have as freelance clients
- I cleared out my desk of all personal items and only left the items belonging to the company I was working for at the time

I even went so far as to put in my two-weeks notice. And two weeks later, I was self-employed and have been ever since. (*Note: I do not recommend quitting your job before you have something else lined up! That is not the right move for everyone, but for me at the time, it was an inspired action I felt called to take, and it ended up working out. That does not mean you will have the same result.*)

Or, for example, let's say you want your boyfriend (or girlfriend) to live with you. Rather than just thinking about it, prepare for it to happen. Clear out space in your closet for him to put his stuff. Get rid of any unnecessary clutter or stuff that's piled up around your house. Buy him his own coffee mug to use in the mornings. Whatever makes you feel like he's moving in with you. That is what it means to prepare to receive.

The more you can prepare to make your quantum leap, the faster it will start to unfold in your life. Whether you prepare a little or a lot, anything you do prepare shows the Universe you're ready for your next level *now*.

Pretend However You Can

As children, we have no problem acting out our deepest and wildest fantasies and believing they're real. But as adults, we underestimate the power of pretending. So, take a cue from your inner child and pretend your quantum leap is a done deal, in whichever ways you can. As I said, the small actions will add up.

For example, let's say you want to quantum leap your vacations, and instead of going to the same places you usually go, you want to go big and take a vacation to Fiji. Not only that, but you specifically want to stay in one of those over-water bungalows at the Fiji Marriott Resort in Momi Bay. You can pretend it's already happening by doing things that make you feel like it is.

Get yourself a notepad and pen from another Marriott hotel and every time you use it, pretend like it's from the Fiji Marriott, or go stay at a local Marriott hotel and pretend you're in Fiji. Update your passport—or get a passport if you don't have one yet, so you're ready to travel to Fiji. Whenever you're outside and feeling the sun warm on your face, close your eyes and imagine you're lounging in your over-water bungalow and feeling the warm Fiji sun instead. Find an over-water bungalow picture from that hotel, and make it the lock screen on your phone; whenever you look at the pic, imagine yourself staying in that bungalow.

The more you can get into action around the things you want—even with small actions—the more you'll start to believe it's really happening.

What Would You Not Be Doing?

Another part of acting as if is looking at what you would *not* be doing. There are likely things you're doing right now that the version of you who has what you want would not do. And that's something to consider as well. Putting a stop to those things also helps you to act as if you already have what you want.

Here's an example. When I was stepping into the identity of being a bestselling author, I realized that something I would not be doing was checking my social media or emails first thing when I woke up. In fact, that version of me wouldn't look at any of that stuff until much later in the day, after her writing was finished. I also knew I wouldn't have notifications on my phone, distracting me with social media messages or text messages all day long. I would be intentional and check my messages when I was ready to and not because a notification forced me to.

Knowing all of the stuff I wouldn't be doing allowed me to put a stop to it. And that helped me to act even more as the version of me who was already a bestselling author.

So, what would the quantum-leaped version of you *not* be doing? If you really think about it, you can come up with a whole list of things. Stopping some of those things are also acting as if actions. And the more things you stop doing, the more you align yourself with being the quantum-leaped version of you.

Now there may be some things you wouldn't be doing as the next-level version of you that you can't stop doing at this time. For example, if you have a day job, but the quantum-leaped version of you would be working for yourself, you may not be able to stop going to your day job right now. But you can at least be clear on what you would stop doing, even if you can't stop all of it just yet. Again, this isn't about having to take every action or having to stop doing everything you wouldn't be doing. But it *is* about stopping what you can stop right now, and letting the rest be an awareness for later when you're closer to closing the gap for yourself.

Who Would You Be?

We talked a little about identity in Chapter One, and this chapter requires a discussion of it as well. Because it's more about who you're being, and who you see yourself as when you're taking the actions than it is about the actions themselves. It's about how you carry yourself. It's about your attitude. And most importantly, it's about your energy.

There's a big energetic difference between fully standing behind every action your take and *knowing* you're becoming the person you want to be and taking an action just because you think you *should*.

If you have a hard time with the identity thing and seeing yourself as this new version of you, here's an exercise that always helps me. I like to think of someone who already has what I want, and then ask myself: *what would that person do?*

For example, while she doesn't have the career I want for myself, Kourtney Kardashian comes to mind when I think about the kind of physical body, health, wellness, lifestyle, relationship, and money I desire to have. So, when I feel like I'm lacking confidence or am not feeling the identity of who I want to be, I'll ask myself, *what would Kourtney do in this situation? What would she say? What would her attitude be? What would she choose to do?*

Now I don't *really* know the answer to this, but I can assume it based on what I know about Kourtney. For example, Kourtney wouldn't let a hater on social media ruin her day. She would stand up for herself, she would maybe even put them in their place. So, I could apply this same identity toward any haters I get on my social media accounts. And when I do this, I'm acting as the quantum-leaped version of me, because I know that version of me wouldn't take any shit on social media either.

I also do this with my favorite authors and screenwriters. I will ask myself, *would Nora Ephron write it like this? Would Sophie Kinsella choose that story idea over this one?* And that helps me to tap into the identity of the next-level version of myself because both of those people have the career that I desire to have.

Identity can be a tough one, especially because we've been taught so many bullshit things about ourselves that aren't true. But you can "hack" your identity and quantum leap yourself to the next level by tapping into the identity, attitude, outlook, etc., of the people you admire and/or the people who already have the things that you want.

Standards and Boundaries

This is a big one when it comes to acting as if because there's a pretty good chance the standards you've had up until now are not the standards you'd have if you were at your next level. You'd most likely have higher standards in many areas of your life. You wouldn't tolerate a lot of the stuff you've been tolerating. You would have boundaries in place to protect yourself, your mindset, your energy, and whatever else in your life needs protection.

When I was making a quantum leap in my love life, from being single to having my dream relationship, I had to raise my standards around men. For far too long, I was settling for less than I desired and deserved because I had an unconscious belief that I wasn't good enough to have the kind of man I wanted. I had one situation in particular that I knew I had to put an end to if I wanted to quantum leap in the area of relationships. There was this guy I'd had an on-and-off thing with since my early 20s. He was my between-relationships guy. I was totally in love with him, but he never felt the same way about me. For him, I was a convenience. He never went out of his way to make time for me, like I did for him. It was always about what he wanted to do, and how he wanted things to be. And something I wasn't willing to admit to myself for almost two decades of this back-and-forth with him was that he was just not that into me.

Yes, he was attracted to me and he liked me as an option. But he was never going to rearrange his life to be with me. This was very hard for me to accept, because I spent so many years of my life pining for him, and hoping and dreaming that one day things would be different for us.

But as I was making my quantum leap in the area of relationships, I knew I had to let him go. I had to cut the energetic tie I had with him for far too long. I had to raise my standards, and know that I deserved better than just being an option or a convenience to someone.

I wanted to be someone's everything. I wanted to be with someone who wanted to be with me just as much, and who was willing to rearrange whatever was needed to make that happen. And when I finally raised my standard in men, love, and relationships, and put an end to anything I had going on that didn't align with that, then and only then did I make a quantum leap into the relationship I had always dreamed of.

So, where have you not been upholding the standards you know you're worthy of? Where in your life have you been tolerating things that you know you would not be putting up with if you were your quantum-leaped self who has the thing(s) you want?

Spend some time really digging into this one, and then raise your standards. Put whatever boundaries in place that are required from now on. You deserve it.

Your Guiding Question

There are a lot of different questions you can ask yourself with regard to acting as if–I've given you a lot of them in this chapter already. But there's one specific question you can use as a guide on a day-to-day, moment-to-moment basis. And that question is, *what would the [insert your quantum leap] version of me do?* In a more specific way, it could look like this: *what would the millionaire version of me do? What would the fit and healthy version of me wear? What would the in-a-dream-relationship version of me choose?* Another way to ask it could be, *would the [insert quantum leap] version of me do this, eat this, take action on this, choose this, etc.?*

You have to get yourself used to thinking, believing, feeling, and then acting from being that person now. You have to get used to asking yourself questions about what and who that version of you would be. That's how you tap into the actions you can begin taking to step into being that person now. And as you do, you'll start to receive inspired ideas for more actions you could take.

So, for example, if you're wanting to make a quantum leap in your health and fitness, you would apply the question, *"what would the fit and healthy version of me do?"* to everything in your daily life. Before you make breakfast, you would ask yourself, *what would the fit and healthy version of me eat for breakfast (or would the fit and healthy version of me eat this)?* And then whatever answer comes to you, that's the action to take. Then when it's time to get dressed for the day, you would ask yourself, *what would the fit and healthy version of me wear today?* And whatever answer comes to you, that's what you wear. You would apply this question to everything all day, every day, and then act upon the answer you receive from asking it.

A big part of this is learning to trust your gut instinct and not questioning it or reasoning your way into choosing something else. Your first instinct–the first answer you get when you ask the question–is almost always right. So go with it.

The more you do that, the more you're closing the gap between who and where you are now, and who and where you want to be.

Plan the Celebration Ahead of Time

In my opinion, celebrating is severely underrated. And that's sad because not only is it fun to celebrate things, but it's also an easy way to create a quantum leap in your life. Back in 2014, when I wanted to have my best month in business, I used celebration to make it happen.

I didn't set any specifics around what my "best month" meant, I just knew I wanted to make the most money I'd made up until that point and enjoy everything I was doing. My favorite restaurant at the time was *The Melting Pot*, but I rarely ate there because it was pricey. So, I decided that's where I wanted to have dinner to celebrate my best month in business ever. And I wanted to bring my then-husband and my mom to dinner with me.

I called the restaurant and made a reservation for a date that was a month away, and then I got to work visualizing it as if it was already done. Every day for four minutes (I set a timer), I would visualize myself having that celebratory dinner. I imagined myself choosing a dress from my closet, putting it on, walking out the door of my apartment, driving to the restaurant, walking up to the hostess and giving my name, walking over to our table, sitting down, ordering food, and toasting my mom and then-husband with a glass of champagne. I imagined this in specific detail every single day that month. Most mornings when my timer went off, I had happy tears pouring down my face because my visualization felt so real to me as if I really had just experienced that celebratory dinner.

As the month went along, things started to happen. I got an

idea to launch a story planning workshop (at the time I was doing book editing and story coaching), and I immediately had a bunch of sign-ups. I got an unexpected book editing client who also wanted to pay me to help her self-publish her book. In total, I made $8,500 cash, which was my highest income month at that point. And then right before the month ended, I was gifted a free $1,500 coaching program from a coach I knew online. I added that into the total for the month and realized I had my first $10k month!

By visualizing the celebration for my best month in business every single day, and in such detail that it created an emotional charge for me, it literally forced the how to show up. Whatever needed to happen to get me to that celebratory dinner happened. And at the end of the month, when I actually went to *The Melting Pot* and had my dinner with my mom and then-husband, it was everything I imagined and more.

I've used pre-planned celebrations to quantum leap myself many times in many different areas of my life and business ever since. It's such a fun and under-utilized way to manifest things. I highly recommend giving it a try. It's a great way to act as if you've already achieved, received and quantum leaped to the outcome that you desire.

Gratitude In Advance

Being grateful in advance for your quantum leap will help make it happen even faster. Advanced gratitude is the ultimate acting as if. It sends a strong message to the Universe that you believe so deeply you will have what you want that you're willing to be grateful for it ahead of time.

Advanced gratitude is one of my secret weapons to manifesting things quickly and quantum leaping over and over again in the different areas of my life. Before I understood how powerful advanced gratitude is, I used to ask the Universe to help me with things. But every time I did that, it felt like I was asking for permission. And that's not required.

You don't need to ask the Universe for things. It doesn't have to grant you permission to have what you want. You get to decide and the Universe helps you make it happen. No permission necessary (other than your own).

Now I just thank the Universe in advance for whatever it is I want, and I know and trust that the Universe is on it and taking care of it for me. I do this with big things—like the areas of my life where I want to quantum leap—and I do it with small things, like getting the best table or waitress at the restaurant I'm about to eat at. Advanced gratitude works with everything.

The phrase I use is, *thank you Universe for [insert the thing you're having advanced gratitude for]*. Some more specific examples:

- Thank you Universe for helping me get a front-row parking spot at the store
- Thank you Universe for sending me an idea for my next book
- Thank you Universe for finding me the exact perfect dress for my friend's wedding next month
- Thank you Universe for helping me to love myself
- Thank you Universe for finding my missing necklace for me

I also have a blanket advanced gratitude statement that I use on a daily basis. This statement has created some serious magic in my life, and I know that it will do the same for you if you decide to use it in your life. That phrase is: *thank you Universe for showing me how good it can get.*

I can think of no better way to act as if than being grateful in advance of your quantum leap happening. The more grateful you are, the more magnetic you become.

An Acting As If Example

I wanted to share with you one of my all-time favorite act as if manifestations. This was an instant manifestation and it's a great example of how acting as if works when you choose to believe and not allow for any other outcome. This story is excerpted from my book, *Miraclefesting*.

How I Manifested A Spot In A Sold-Out 9:30 A.M. SoulCycle Class

One Friday night in 2017, my friend invited me to join her for SoulCycle at 9:30 a.m. the next morning. I'd been wanting to try SoulCycle out for months so I was super excited that she invited me.

The only problem was... the 9:30 a.m. class was full.

This is where most people would get stopped. But I'm not most people.

I decided right there in that moment I would be in the 9:30 a.m. class with my friend.

So I paid for a class credit on the SoulCycle app and then clicked on "join the waitlist" for the class my friend was in, letting the Universe know I planned on being there.

The message on the app said if a spot opened in the class, they'd call people from the waitlist in the order they signed up. Otherwise, the class was full and the credit would be returned back to my account.

This is as far as most people would go. They'd buy the class, put their name on the waitlist, and then they'd wait.

But, again, I'm not most people.

I know that in order to manifest something you want, you have to not only be committed to the end result--getting into the class--but you have to wear blinders to all other possibilities, and you have to act as if whatever you want is already yours. So that's exactly what I did.

Immediately after I signed up for the class, I located my gym clothes in the hamper and washed them, because I needed something to wear for the class.

Then I packed my bag for the morning because I wanted to have a change of clothes for after class, plus I packed my journal and a pen so I had something to do before the class started.

Next, I looked up where the closest parking garage to the SoulCycle studio was, so I knew exactly where to park when I arrived.

My plan was to show up 30 minutes before the class started and wait there for a spot to open. Because I fully believed that spot was already mine.

In the morning, I woke up at 7:40 a.m., threw on my gym clothes, took my dog for a walk, set up the slow-cooker for dinner, and then I grabbed the bag I packed the night before and I was off to SoulCycle to wait for my spot to open.

Just as I was pulling out of the parking space at my apartment complex to drive downtown, my phone started ringing. It was the SoulCycle studio calling to let me know a spot had opened in the 9:30 a.m. class.

Not only did I manifest my spot in the class with my friend, but since I was already up-and-about, I decided to grab a green smoothie downtown and do some journaling before class began.

Everything worked out exactly as I wanted it to because I was willing to go above and beyond what most people would do.

Most people would've been stopped by the class being full. Most people would've stayed in bed and waited for SoulCycle to call them and let them know a spot had opened.

But if I had done either of those things, I wouldn't have gotten into the class.

I acted as if the spot was already a sure thing and did everything I would've done if it was. That's why I got into the class and got to experience SoulCycle for the first time, along with my friend who invited me to be there.

You can absolutely have, do and be anything you set your mind to. Anything!!

But you have to be willing to do the work, to take the actions, and to act in faith that what you want is already yours.

THE MORE YOU take the act as if actions that feel aligned for you, the more you're stepping into the identity of already being the person who has what you want and who has made a quantum leap in the area(s) you desire to. Who you're being, and your identity is what it's really all about. When you identify as that version of you, you will eventually become it (this is also known as the Law of Assumption).

A Brainstorm of Acting As If Actions

On my TikTok channel @fuckthehow, one of the main things people ask me for is specific ideas for acting as if actions. I've given you a lot of in-general information in this chapter, plus provided examples to help illustrate this for you. But I wanted to go a step further and brainstorm some specific act as if actions for the top three life areas where most people want to make a quantum leap: money, love, and physical body.

Keep in mind these are just ideas and examples of potential acting as if actions. Your actions may be different based on what you specifically want. Also, there are no guarantees that taking any of these actions will cause you to quantum leap. I am simply providing a list of ideas to inspire you as you begin your acting as if journey.

Potential Acting As If Money Actions:

- Open a new checking or savings account so more money has a place to go
- Any time you spend money, do it from a place of gratitude and belief that there's more where that came from
- Start setting aside a specific amount of money every week into a "dream life fund" (SmartyPig is a good tool for this)
- Figure out how much it would cost for you to have your dream life–actually sit down and price out the monthly car payment, the house payment, what you would save and/or donate every month, etc. Whatever you would be spending money on in your dream life, figure out what the monthly cost of that is. Now you have a specific figure to aim for.
- Stop spending money on things that don't make you happy
- Give away a small percentage of your income to a charity or cause you care about

Potential Acting As If Love Life Actions:

- Create a playlist of uplifting love songs and listen to it on repeat, feeling into the emotions of having the love life you desire

- Watch movies and/or TV shows that portray the type of love life you want and feel into the emotions of having it now
- Take yourself on a date
- Treat yourself how you'd like your significant other to treat you
- Buy yourself flowers
- Love yourself
- Create the kind of relationship with yourself that you'd like to have with your significant other
- Make space in your life, your schedule, and/or your heart for the love you desire
- Heal any old wounds and baggage about men (or women), love, relationships, etc.

Potential Acting As If Physical Body Actions:

- Dress how you'd dress if you already had the body you want
- Buy yourself some new clothes
- Find a type of workout that you absolutely love and commit to doing it
- Build a consistent habit of exercising
- Treat your body like a queen (or king)
- Talk to yourself and your body like you're speaking to someone you love
- Implement new food, fitness, and/or self-talk standards and stick with them
- Join a gym
- Hire a trainer

Quantum Leap Your Life: Chapter Five Recap

- **How can you start to act in faith of receiving what you want?**—another way to look at it would be, how can you prepare to receive what you want? Make a list of everything you could do, and then choose something from that list and go do it today. Repeat again tomorrow.
- **What would you be doing if you were already the person who has the thing(s) you want?**—what would your life be like? And how can you start to bring some of that into your life right now through action?
- **Who can you use as a living-proof example and channel their identity, attitude, energy, actions, etc.?**—choose someone who has the thing(s) and/or outcome that you want for yourself and then play pretend. Have fun with this.
- **What would you no longer be doing if you were already the version of you who has what you want?**—this is a question worth thinking about because there are probably things you're doing right now that you can stop doing in order to put yourself into alignment–energetically and physically–with the version of you who already has what you want.
- **What boundaries and standards would you have in place if you were already there?**—what specific areas would you raise your standards in and/or create a boundary around?
- **Choose a "guiding question" that is specific to the quantum leap you want to make and use it all day every day**—use the "Your Guiding Question" section above to formulate this question for yourself.
- **Plan your quantum leap celebration in advance**—be sure to visualize yourself experiencing that celebration

every single day for at least three to five minutes. Connect to the emotions you'd be feeling as much as possible when you do this. Visualizing forces "the how" to show up for you.

Quantum Leap Your Life: Chapter Five Journal Prompts

For each of these prompts, do some freestyle journaling, or answer in bullet points, whichever works best for you.

- What would it look like if you were one hundred percent all in on being the version of you who already has the thing(s) you want?
- What would you be doing if you weren't worried about becoming that person or having that thing?
- Why would you not want to go all in on your quantum leap? What might stand in your way?
- If you were doing everything you could to make your quantum leap a reality, what would that look like for you?
- Who would you love to be more like, in identity, lifestyle, attitude, actions, etc., and how can you start being more like them right now?

SIX

IT TAKES AS LONG AS IT TAKES

If you've done everything we've talked about so far and are believing, feeling, thinking, and acting like the quantum-leaped version of you–congratulations. You are now a vibrational match to being that person and having the things that person has. Now you just have to keep it up until the shift happens in your physical reality.

Your quantum leap begins on the inside. Your thoughts and beliefs are different. You start feeling like a different version of yourself. Once enough change has occurred on the inside, you start to notice your actions changing on the outside. You're suddenly doing things you weren't doing before, or you start to notice that it doesn't feel hard to take the actions you've been wanting to take. You just take them automatically, almost like a habit has been created out of nowhere.

When all of that starts happening, you know the changes in your physical reality aren't far behind. But how long it takes for your physical reality to change varies from person to person, and depends on many factors that are out of your control.

With every quantum leap, there are always things in the energetic and spiritual realm, as well as the physical realm, that need to be rearranged, changed, shifted, removed, aligned, etc.

So, it may take time before things start to happen, especially if where you are right now is very different than where you desire to be. Relax and give the Universe space to do its work.

Surrender To Divine Timing

Timing seems to be a huge hangup for most people when it comes to quantum leaping and manifesting. We tend to try and control the timing of things, and that's not your job in the manifestation process. Timing is the Universe's job (for more on your job versus the Universe's, be sure to read my book, *F*ck the How*).

So yes, you can have an idea of when you want something to happen, but if it doesn't happen by then, so be it. Don't make it mean anything, and don't stop what you've been doing.

So many people give up on their quantum leap rather than seeing it through to the end because it's taking too long. But the truth is, it doesn't always happen in the timing that you think it should, and so you have to be in it for the long haul and be willing to stick with it and do whatever it takes until it happens.

You have to be fully committed to getting what you want and being who you want to be. So committed that nothing will stop you, including it not happening in the time you want it to. Giving up is one of the top reasons people don't get to be or have what they want.

You have to decide that it hasn't happened YET, not that it isn't going to happen. There's a huge energetic difference between the two. One says you've essentially given up and are looking for evidence to back that decision, the other says that you still believe.

The other thing to remember is that your human self really has no idea how long it takes to make something happen. And the divine timeline is often a lot faster than yours. So, you could be making what you want take even longer by putting your expectations on it, instead of surrendering to the timeline of the Universe.

Repeat after me: *My quantum leap takes as long as it takes.*

The Truth About Quantum Leaping

Whatever quantum leap you desire to make, there will always be a journey from where you are to where you want to be. You need to learn to stick with it. You have to build up your inner strength and resilience so that you can handle–and even enjoy–the journey. If you can't do that, it really won't matter if you make your quantum leap or not.

Your quantum leap is not an "end point" where you can just rest on your laurels. There will always be things to maintain.

Like being in a relationship, for example. Once you find the person you want to be with, you don't just stop. You have to continue to build and grow and develop that relationship, otherwise, you're not going to have it for very long. Same thing with your dream physical body. You could go on a diet and exercise more to get the body you want, but you'll still have to maintain a certain way of eating and working out if you want to keep it.

Same thing with your money, your business, your career, your lifestyle, your family, your possessions, or any area that you want to make a quantum leap in. There will always be something to maintain. Even if it's not something physical, you will still be maintaining the mindset, thoughts, beliefs, and feelings that got you to your quantum leap.

And once you get where you want to be, there will inevitably be somewhere else you want to go. You will always have a new desire show up after another is achieved. So, if you're not enjoying the journey, you're missing the whole point. It's always about the journey. The journey is the destination.

Fuck Your Physical Reality

You have to stop letting your physical reality take you out of the game. Your current physical reality that you see and experience every day is simply the effect of your previous ways of thinking, believing, feeling, and acting. Your inner world is the cause, your outer world is the effect.

That doesn't mean your physical reality won't eventually change. It absolutely will, as you trust and keep going. But until it does change, you have to not put so much weight into what you're seeing or experiencing, or what's showing up. Your current physical reality is old news.

Don't rely on your physical reality for evidence that your quantum leap is happening. Especially in the early stages when there is likely to be little to no physical evidence. Doing so can mean death to your quantum leap.

The more you believe your current reality is all there is, the more you will get what is, over and over again. It's a Groundhog Day that there's seemingly no escape from. The only way out is to go inside yourself, make changes, and then hold on tight until you see those same changes reflected in your physical reality.

If you allow yourself to be swayed by what you see in your current physical reality, you'll never create a strong enough belief that things are changing.

The majority of your quantum leap happens in the quantum, meaning the invisible, energetic realm that you can't see with your physical senses. But it's still there, and it's very real. The more you believe, trust, and put your faith in that, the more you'll start to see the quantum reveal itself in the physical.

Signs Are Cool, But Not Required

The Universe often uses "signs" to confirm for us that things are happening in the quantum, even though we can't always see those things in our physical realities yet. The types of signs will vary and will depend upon what feels like a sign for you.

For some people, the Universe sends repeating sets of numbers, like 111, 222, 777, 888, or 1111, 4444, etc. For others, it sends bird feathers, butterflies, or ladybugs. For others, it sends pennies or dimes that you randomly find. And for others, it may send something else. You may also receive a combination of these things.

Sometimes there will be no signs at all, and the only thing you have to go on is how you feel internally. This is why–more than anything else–you must learn to trust how you feel inside of yourself. If you're feeling good, you're on the path to your quantum leap. If you're feeling like what you want is possible, you're believing in it, and you're thinking in alignment with having it, then you're on the path to your quantum leap. If you're acting as if, even in a small way, you're on the path to your quantum leap.

Be grateful when you do receive signs, but don't rely on them in order to continue believing. The more you depend on them, the more you'll push them away. You must believe in your quantum leap regardless of whether you see any signs or not.

Truthfully, signs really have no meaning except the meaning you give them. You can definitely use signs as confirmation of what you want, or that you're on the right path, or to help you make a decision, or whatever you decide to use them for. But don't let the sign be the most important thing.

Trust and Keep Going

You must always and forever trust and keep going. No matter what happens or doesn't happen. No matter what your physical reality looks like right now. No matter how long it takes. No matter if you're seeing changes, results, or not.

How do you trust and keep going? You keep on deciding to. You keep on acting as if. You keep on thinking, believing, and feeling in alignment with what you want. You continue to prepare for its inevitable arrival. You continue to remind yourself of the *Four Truths of Surrender* (from Chapter One).

Don't give yourself permission to quit. Don't let yourself get pulled off your path. And if you find that you've taken a detour and stopped being a vibrational match to what you want, make yourself aware of it as quickly as you can and then get right back on track.

Doing all of these things will ensure that your quantum leap is a done deal.

Quantum Leap Your Life: Chapter Six Recap

- **How can you begin to surrender to divine timing?** —rather than trying to determine the timeline, surrender it to the Universe, knowing that you always get to have what you want or something even better, no matter how long it takes. Then allow the Universe to deliver it to you in the perfect divine timing.
- **How can you enjoy the journey more?**—the journey to your quantum leap is the whole point because once you arrive at the place you want to be, there will be another dream or desire to fulfill. The more you can enjoy the journey, the happier you'll be during the process.
- **Give yourself permission to ignore your physical reality as much as possible, until it begins to look more like you want it to**—until then, don't give too much weight to what you're seeing or experiencing.
- **What signs has the Universe been showing you as confirmation that your quantum leap is happening?** —keep track of it in a journal or on your phone. Whenever you need reassurance, return back to the list of signs you've received and remember that it's always

working, even when you think it's not (especially when you think it's not).

- **How can you begin to use the *Four Truths of Surrender* in your daily life?**—go back to Chapter One and write these four truths down on a Post-it, and then hang it in your home or workspace, to reference whenever you need reminding.

Quantum Leap Your Life: Chapter Six Journal Prompts

For each of these prompts, do some freestyle journaling, or answer in bullet points, whichever works best for you.

- What would it look like for me if I was truly in surrender and not worrying about making my quantum leap?
- If I was enjoying the journey, what would I be doing?
- What provisions can I put in place whenever I find myself worrying or doubting my quantum leap?

PLEASE LEAVE A REVIEW ON AMAZON

Dear Reader,

I just wanted to say **thank you so much for reading and supporting this book**.

As an independent, self-published author, it really helps me spread the word and get this book into more hands when you leave a review.

So if you could **head over to www.jenniferblanchard.net/ quantumleap** (link goes directly to the book's Amazon page) **and leave me a review, it would mean the world to me.**

Dream life or bust,
Jennifer Blanchard

A FREE DIGITAL COURSE FOR YOU

Act Like It: A Digital Course

By purchasing *Quantum Leap Your Life*, you get FREE access to **Act Like It**, my six-module digital course all about how to act as if your way into anything you desire and dream of.

It's the perfect accompaniment to this book, especially if you like to listen to the concepts I've talked about over and over again. Each module includes an audio training + worksheet.

Here's how to claim your free course:

1. **Go to: www.jenniferblanchard.net/actlikeitfreebie**
    2. **You will automatically be redirected to a Dropbox folder** that contains all of the digital course content
    3. **You can choose to use the course in the cloud, or download a copy to you computer**

Any questions? Email: support@jenniferblanchard.net

THE MANIFESTING TRIFECTA

You have this book... and now it's time to also add *F*ck the How* and *Manifest Everything* to your library. Those books work together with *Quantum Leap Your Life* to give you an even deeper understanding of the spiritual and energetic concepts that will help you manifest more intentionally.

I consider *Quantum Leap Your Life* to be a foundational read for anyone who wants to manifest intentionally.

But if you want to deepen your understanding, see more examples, and embody the elements of this process even further, then *F*ck the How* and *Manifest Everything* will round out your Manifesting Trifecta.

And here's a sneak peek at both of those books:

F*CK THE HOW

What If Not Knowing How Was No Longer An Obstacle To Your Dreams and Desires?

The number one reason you're not going for your deepest dreams and desires in life--or even giving yourself full permission to want those things--is because you don't know How you'll make them a reality. Not knowing How then becomes a barrier that stops you from doing, being, or having the things and the life you know you're meant for.

But the truth is, you never, ever, ever, ever need to know How you'll do, be, or have something before you decide that you're going to. No matter what it is you desire and dream of. Even if it's a so-called "pipe dream."

You don't need to know all of the steps. You don't need a strategy or an action plan. You don't have to make a to-do list and check everything off. You don't even have to do most of what you think it takes to do, be, and have what you want.

You just have to do your part and stay the hell out of the way so the Universe can do its part.

F*ck the How demystifies manifestation and teaches you the process to go from dream or desire in your heart to actually receiving it in your real, physical life, without ever having to know How beforehand.

Whether you're a creative with big dreams, an over-thinker, a control freak, or someone who just gets way too caught up on the How of making your desires happen, this paradigm-shifting book will help you to set the How aside and get any-freaking-thing that you want.

F*ck the How is available in eBook, paperback, and Audible

MANIFEST EVERYTHING

It's Time For You To Have Your Version of "It All"

Do you feel like you're meant for more than the life you're currently living?

- *Does seeing someone else having what you want cause serious FOMO?*
- *Do you see a bigger vision for yourself and your life but don't know how to reach it?*
- *Do you believe that you're too old (or too young) or that it's too late to have the life you dream of?*
- *Or, are you simply just looking for a better way to have more of what you want more of the time?*

In *Manifest Everything*, Author Jennifer Blanchard teaches you her signature 8-step methodology for manifesting whatever you want without ever worrying about how you'll do it.

MANIFEST is an acronym for this method where each letter represents one step in the process. Here's what it looks like:

M - Massive clarity

A - Advance gratitude

N - Now decide you're worthy

I - Inner work

F - Feel it

E - Embody it

S - Show up for your life

T - Take inspired action

The first time she shared this process on her TikTok channel, the video got tens of thousands of views, and someone even commented and said it was *"about a hundred books and thousands of dollars in manifesting courses distilled down into the best process flow I've ever heard."*

Manifest Everything has two parts within it:

- Part one explains the 8-step methodology and shows an example of applying this method to manifesting love
- Part two is a workbook that walks you through everything to ask yourself and/or consider for each of the 8 steps

When you apply this manifesting process in your life, you can learn to manifest whatever you want--including love, money, better health, a car, a house, increased business, and anything else you desire. There are no limits to what's possible!!

—> Go to: www.dreamlifeorbust.com to complete your Manifesting Trifecta today!

ACKNOWLEDGMENTS

Thank you to my readers for picking up this book and reading all the way to the end. I know your life will be immensely better for doing so. Thank you to my amazing boyfriend, Dave, for always celebrating with me and giving me the space I need for my writing and creative pursuits. Thank you to my longtime friend and editor, Mary DeRosa, for helping me to make this book the best it could possibly be. Thank you to all of the amazing people who follow me on my @fuckthehow TikTok channel—your comments and questions on my videos have inspired so much of what I've written on these pages.

ABOUT THE AUTHOR

Jennifer Blanchard is the self-made bestselling author of *F*ck the How, Quantum Leap Your Life, and Manifest Everything*, which are roadmaps for manifesting your dreams and desires without needing to know the How ahead of time.

Her practical approach to intentional manifesting is doable and easy to understand. Readers of her books and students of her courses have said Jennifer clarifies and expands on everything they've previously learned about manifestation.

She has a Bachelor's degree in Journalism and Public Relations with a minor in Creative Writing.

Jennifer has authored more than a dozen books, including several works of fiction, and is co-author of the book, *Miraclefesting: Inspiring Stories to Help You Recognize and Create Everyday Miracles In Your Life*.

facebook.com/dreamlifeorbust

instagram.com/thefeelgoodlife

youtube.com/jenniferblanchard

amazon.com/stores/Jennifer-Blanchard/author/B091RH6JCR

tiktok.com/@fuckthehow

Made in the USA
Coppell, TX
12 November 2024

40139332R00066